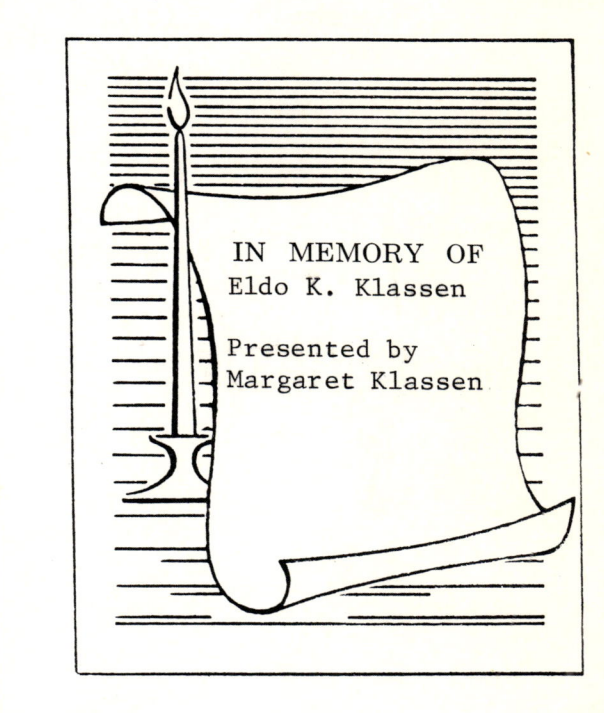

THE CHURCH

REACHING OUT

C. **Burtt Potter**

FOREWORD by OWEN COOPER

MOORE PUBLISHING COMPANY
Durham, North Carolina 27705

Copyright 1976 by Moore Publishing Company, Durham, North Carolina. All rights reserved. Printed in the United States of America.

Library of Congress Catalog Card Number: 76-12219.
ISNB 0-87716-062-7

*Dedicated to my parents
Burtt and Marion Potter,
for giving me life, unfailing
love, and academic and
theological education,
motivation to excell, and
constant encouragement.*

PUBLISHER'S NOTE

The church is encouraged if not commanded to reach out. Both congregations and ministers need the innovative changes that keeps the church dynamic. This is neither to say nor imply that the Word changes because the Word is our greatest source of constancy. Yet within the framework of the Word and within the shadow of the Cross, Christians need to reassess and refurbish in order to keep their witness alive and their faith vibrant.

This book is filled with experiences, of the author and others, that result from innovation in technique. New paths are shown to those who may have not travelled traditional pathways; still they lead to the Kingdom of God. And that's what it's all about.

Evangelism, its work and spirit, is everywhere and touches everybody. It is the essence of *The Church Reaching Out*. It is our way of sharing, after we have defined human needs and discovered those that are unmet.

If we know this as God's world and wish to overcome our provincialism, if we wish to be more selfless than selfish, and if we believe the Word is applicable to all humans, we'll find Burtt Potter challenging and provocative as he gives us guidelines in *The Church Reaching Out*.

Eugene V. Grace, M.D.
Publisher

CONTENTS

Foreword by Owen Cooper
Introduction

I. THE SURGE OF BOLD EVANGELISM, 1

II. ONE-TO-ONE, PERSON-TO-PERSON ENCOUNTERS, 15
   Telephone, 15
      Counseling, 15
      Crises Center, 16
      Follow-up To Television Broadcast, 18
      Telephone Survey, 18
      Prayer Service, 20
      Recorded Devotionals, 20
      Referrals, 20
   Personal Services, 21
      Medical, 21
         Well-Baby, 21 Medical, 22
         Cooperation with Health Agencies, 23
         Planned Parenthood Clinic, 23
      Food Distribution, 24
      Housing, 26
         Youth, 26
         Family, 26
         Retirement, 27
      Legal, 27
      Educational, 28
         Tutoring, 29
         Literacy, 30
      Clothing Distribution, 30
      Ministry to Newcomers, 31
      Family Ministries, 32
         Big Brothers/Big Sisters, 32
         Babysitting, 32
      Vocational Placement, 33

III. SMALL GROUP APPROACHES, 35
   Classes, 35
      Household Hints, 35
         Homemaking, 35

  Nutrition, 35
  Cooking, 36
  Money Management, 36
  Grooming, 36
  Sewing, 37
 Health, 38
  Exercise, 38
  Alcohol, 39
   Alcoholics Anonymous, 39
   Bible Class, 39
  Drug Treatment, 40
   Gradual Withdrawal, 40
   Immediate Withdrawal, 41
  Therapy, 41
 Vocation, 42
  Church-Staffed & Sponsored Classes, 42
   Mechanics Class, 42
   Key-Punch Class, 43
   Typing Class, 43
   Plumbing Class, 44
   General Para-Professional Classes, 44
   Teaching Classes, 44
  Church-Initiated Classes With Government Staffing, 44
  Church-Initiated Classes With Private Funding, 45
  Church Membership Classes, 46
  Children's Education, 47
   Sesame Street Classes, 47
   Head Start Classes, 48
   Day Care Classes, 48
  Drama, 49
 Clubs, 50
  Recreation, 50
  Parents Without Partners, 51
  Hobby Classes, 51
   Ceramics, 51
   Chess, 51
   Quilting, 52
   Arts and Crafts, 53
   Photography, 53
   Dominoes, 53
   Skydiving, 53
   Ham Radio, 54
  Athletics, 54
   Weight-Lifting, 54
   Bowling, 54
   Basketball, 54

IV. INNOVATIVE INDOOR MINISTRIES, 56
  Conversing, 56
    Bible Fellowship Studies, 56
      Military Base, 58
      Offshore Oil Rig, 58
      College Classroom, 58
      Night Club, 59
      Ranch House, 59
      Business Building, 59
      Apartments, 59
      City Homes, 60
      Church Basement, 60
    Coffeehouse, 61
      Beach House, 61
      Village House, 61
      City House, 61
      Storefront Building, 62
      Church Basement, 62
  Studying, 63
    Reading Room Concept, 63
    Library Ministry, 63
    Book Store Ministry, 63
    Book Review, 64
    Sunday School, 64
    Vacation Bible School, 66
      Local Church Building, 66
  Counseling, 66
    Shopping Centers, 66
    Race Track, 67
    Apartments, 67
    Jails, 67
    Y.M.C.A., 68
    Night Clubs, 68
    Hotels, 68
  Feeding, 69
  Performing, 69
    Church Building, 69
      Style Show, 69
    Restaurant, 70
      Musical Presentations, 70
    Lounge, 70
      Musical Presentations, 70
    Night Club, 70
  Playing, 71
    Shopping Center, 71

    Church Property, 71
    Center, 72
  Worshipping, 72
    Church Building, 72
    Theaters, 73
    Night Clubs, 73
    Shopping Centers, 74
    Race Tracks, 74
      Horse Race Ministry, 74
      Race Car Ministry, 74
    School Auditorium, 75
      High School, 75
      College, 75
CREATIVE OUTDOOR MINISTRIES, 76
  Recreational Programs, 76
    Neighborhood Recreation Programs, 76
    Bible School at Catholic Site, 78
    Ongoing Park Program, 78
    Athletic Clinics, 78
    Race Track Ministry, 79
    Ministry at Camp Grounds, 79
      Sing-A-Long, 79
      Motion Pictures, 79
    Beach Sharing, 80
      Rap Sessions, 80
      Making Friends Informally, 80
      Day Camp, 80
    Youth Happening, 80
      Piano Drop, 80
      Ecology Rock Festival, 81
    Skating Party, 81
    State Fair Performances, 81
  Worship, 82
    Beaches, 82
    Race Tracks, 82
    Parking Lots, 83
    Golf Course, 83
    Marketplace, 83
    Shopping Center, 83
    City Park, 84
    Drive-In Church, 85
    Drive-In Theater, 85
VI. MOBILE MINISTRIES, 87
  Mobile "Transporting" Ministries, 87
    Transporting to Church, 87

  Transporting Taxi Ministry, 89
  Transporting City Tours, 90
  Transporting Float Ministry, 90
 Mobile "Peforming" Ministries, 91
  Puppet Show, 91
  Ventriloquism and Motion Pictures, 91
  Gingerbread House, 92
 Mobile "Delivering" Ministry, 93
  Books, 93
  Recreation, 93
  Medical Help, 93
 Mobile Facility as Meeting Place, 93
  Branch Sunday School, 93
  Youth Bible Fellowship Study, 93
  Trailer Park Activity, 94
  Anti-Occult Unit, 94
  Worship Facility, 94
  Counseling Service, 95

VII. NON-PERSONAL CONFRONTATIONS (Electronics), 97
 Radio, 97
  Religious News, 98
  Devotionals, 99
  Worship, 101
  Spot Announcements, 102
  Panel Discussions, 103
  Music Presentations, 104
  Interviews, 104
 Television, 105
  Variety, 105
  Spot Announcements, 105
  Drama, 105
  Cartoons, 106
  One-Minute Sermon, 106
  Worship, 107
  Secular Talk Show, 108
 Motion Pictures, 108
  Occasional Church Showings, 108 Film Revival, 108
  Films at Fair Pavillions, 109
  Christian Films in Theaters, 109
  Films in Christian-Owned Theaters, 110
  Secular Films in Theaters, 110
 Computers, 111
  Geographical Visitation Matchups, 112
  Interest Matchup for Visitation, 113

Cassette Tape Recordings, 113
　　　Inter-Communication System, 114
VIII. NON-PERSONAL CONFRONTATIONS (Literature), 115
　　　Newspaper, 115
　　　　　Advertisements, 116
　　　　　News Stories, 117
　　　　　Columns, 117
　　　　　Cartoon Messages, 118
　　　Books, 118
　　　　　Christian Book Stores, 119
　　　　　Church Libraries, 119
　　　　　Bookmobiles, 120
　　　　　Church Publication of Pastor's Message, 120
　　　Magazines, 121
　　　Mail-Outs, 121
　　　　　Follow-Up, 122
　　　　　Holiday Scripture Mail-Outs, 122
　　　　　Member Mailouts to Prospects, 122
　　　Tracts, 123
　　　Correspondence Bible Course, 125
IX. HOW THE CHURCH GETS STARTED, 126
　　　Sunday School, 126
　　　The Missions Committee, 128
　　　Women's Missionary Union, 131
　　　Brotherhood, 132
　　　Church Training, 133
Appendix, 139
Footnotes, 162

FOREWORD

I am delighted to contribute this Foreword to *The Church Reaching Out*. The book is timely! It should be an invaluable tool for pastors and mission-minded laymen.

I first met the author, Burtt Potter, during my initial term as President of the Southern Baptist Convention. Burtt was serving as the Area Superintendent of Missions for the state of Nebraska. He invited me to visit Nebraska and address both the Eastern and Western Nebraska Baptist Associations. It was my intention during my two terms as president to visit as many mission fields, both home and foreign as possible. Therefore, I was delighted to accept his invitation and tour the state with him. I observed something quite fresh and exciting in Nebraska. I have had this same sensation in the Northern Plains Convention, and elsewhere in areas where Southern Baptist work is comparatively new. Churches in the North are unable to rely on a steady flow of Southern Baptists transferring their membership, as is customary in the South. For them, church growth is dependent upon the conversion of the indigenous population. They also bear the additional handicap that I have often mentioned elsewhere; native northerners are seldom attracted to the regional implications in the name of their denomination — Southern Baptist Convention.

Evangelistic endeavors seem to be accentuated in these northern Southern Baptist congregations. Out of necessity these churches have searched for and implemented new approaches to cultivate unbelievers for the Kingdom of God. These pastors and denominational workers have received the best in training for their difficult tasks. The skilled staff of the Home Mission Board has vigorously equipped them to proclaim the Gospel with unlimited tangible expressions of God's love.

I am convinced that pastors and congregations in the South can learn from these creative evangelical ministries. It is as if Southern Baptists have vividly learned Jesus' lesson about casting one's bread upon the waters. Churches across the southland have sacrificially given to the cause of missions in our homeland for over a century. Now, these congregations which are frequently subsidized by the Cooperative Program and Annie Armstrong Easter offerings have discovered exciting approaches for stimulating a cynical and indifferent generation to a vital faith in Christ. These new tools for ministry are an answer to prayer.

Southern cities have recently experienced the deterioration that was initially felt in the North. The simplistic approaches of the past are no longer adequate for the complex spiritual problems of today. It may well be that our mission churches in the North have been guided by God to provide relevant solutions for congregations in Atlanta, Birmingham, Memphis, New Orleans, Dallas, Houston and elsewhere in the South.

I recommend this book to individuals and churches who are seriously seeking to win men to a saving faith in Jesus Christ. But I warn you, it is not for those squeamish about hard work. Neither is it for the congregation that is locked-in to traditional methods only.

The Church Reaching Out serves as a manual with a storehouse of innovative ministries. Burtt had the distinction of being the first Southern Baptist missionary to Philadelphia, Pa. He has included many ministries that he personally attempted. He gleaned the others from the successful efforts of missionaries he knew, and his reading of mission work in many denominations. He currently serves as a Sunday School consultant for the North Carolina Convention of Baptists. He has added new insights in Sunday School work that supplement the mission methodology. This provides a helpful blending with the best from both agencies.

I feel there are three stages through which church mission committees, Sunday School councils, or WMU and Brotherhood councils should pass. They need to survey their church fields to uncover specific human needs that have not been met. Then the committees should study this book for possible ministries to meet those needs. The study groups should prayerfully weigh the problems and possible solutions. The Holy Spirit will certainly lead committed Christians to select the specific ministries that are appropriate for their congregation.

May God expand your visions of evangelistic urgency beyond the walls of your church and to the ends of the universe.

OWEN COOPER

President, Southern Baptist Convention
1972-73, 1973-74

INTRODUCTION

This is the book I wish I'd had when I started serving as the first Southern Baptist missionary in Philadelphia in 1966. The complexity of human needs made it difficult for me to know where to get started with my task. The more traditional methods I had used in the South were not adequate for dealing with the diversity of problems and obstacles in the nation's fourth largest city.

I labored for several years, quite satisfied with the little victories we experienced in reaching people for Christ and the church. But Wendell Belew and Jack Redford of the Home Mission Board were able to equip me, as they had hundreds of others, to multiply the effectiveness of my efforts. They explained the diversity of ways that I could touch the lives of desperate people with the love of God. From that point on our ministries seemed to have a more dynamic intensity.

I became the Area Superintendent of Missions for Nebraska Baptists in 1971. Pastors turned to me for help in developing innovative ministries. Many of these ministers had experienced meager evangelistic results and disappointing church growth, despite their dedication to Christ. I began compiling the material in this book to assist those men in their efforts. The actual writing began in October 1972 when I was in a week of revival services in the small Western Nebraska Panhandle community of Chappell.

Many of these illustrations contain ministries used by personal friends around the country or myself. Countless other examples came from beyond Baptist circles. Billy Graham spoke of the relevance of gleaning ideas for ministry from other denominations at the 1972 Southern Baptist Convention. He said, "Many of the programs...in other groups could be adapted to the work of Southern Baptists. It just may be...that God is using somebody else to develop ideas that Southern Baptists could use."

There are several basic observations I'd discovered through my ministries, as well as those of others included in this book. First, unchurched people tend to respond to a church that touches their lives with tangible expressions of love. Denominational labels tend to be insignificant. Certainly, no native Philadelphian or Omaha resident ever turned to our churches *because* of the Southern Baptist label. Second, the only limitation any church has to serving Christ is the limits of its own vision. Congregations that meet human need most fully are those that break through traditional barriers with a diversity of ministries.

When this book was originally completed in 1972 there was no other book with such an extensive compilation of ministries. However, in recent years several books have listed a similar series of approaches. The uniqueness of this book is in the actual documented situations in which individuals and congregations utilized their ministries.

Another helpful feature of the book is the provision of five optional ways that a local church might implement the ministries through existing organizations with greatest effectiveness. These aids are included in the final chapter.

Also, the comprehensive Appendix furnishes other printed material that the reader may turn to for additional information on any given ministry. Obviously, the Appendix will need revision as soon as a single minister relocates. However, the reader can write the minister at the address given, and have it forwarded to his new residence. In other instances the ministry that a pastor developed may have continued after his departure. In these cases a current member of the church staff can answer any questions you might raise.

This book is intended to help both pastors and lay leaders who are dissatisfied with evangelistic results and rate of church growth. It is provided to enable the sensitive Christian who has discovered human need to respond with maximum compassion.

I'm grateful to my fantastic children, Chris and Cara Lynn, who seemed to always understand when Daddy was too busy typing to play games and tell bedtime stories. My wife, Sara, is the "greatest." She edited out hundreds of errors in 1972, and then edited it all again to update it in 1975. Her encouragement carried me through. Her father, Dr. George M. Leiby, helped me get some of the chapters typed. Others whom I appreciate for typing assistance are Mrs. Jo Cress in Omaha and Mrs. Nelda Henry in Raleigh.

I'm indebted to Dr. Gene Grace of Moore Publishing Company for his confidence in publishing the book. Also, I thank my friend, Dan Euliss, for designing the book jacket. An important word of appreciation goes to that great servant of Christ and friend of Baptist mission work, Owen Cooper. His foreword is a major addition to the book and I thank him for it. I also express thanks to my co-worker Douglas Cole of the Baptist State Convention of North Carolina for his counsel on several revisions in the book.

I'm very grateful to the Home Mission Board for nearly eight years of service as a missionary in Philadelphia and throughout Nebraska. They equipped me to see new ways to minister for Christ. I'm indebted to the Baptist State Convention of North Carolina also, for the privilege of sharing many of these concepts to church leaders in my Sunday School conferences.

THE SURGE OF BOLD EVANGELISM

God's challenge to the church is the conversion of the world! Nearly 2000 years ago the Christian church set out with the central purpose of helping God make men truly whole. Churches have done this by leading men to the transformed life that comes from a personal decision to trust and follow Christ. That commitment provides a man transformed life in the Kingdom of God, now and forever.

How successful are Baptist churches today in this evangelistic imperative? Few congregations can boast of any revolutionary conversion harvests in their communities. Church doors are closing throughout the nation. These dying churches are both rural, and urban in setting. They include conservative, as well as liberal congregations. Perplexed Christians ask with bewilderment, "What's the problem? Where have we gone wrong?"

There are a variety of possible shortcomings in evaluating a church's declining evangelistic effectiveness. A vibrant relationship with the living Christ is an indispensable element for effective Christian witnessing. He alone transforms the believer in the image of Himself. There is no other way for an individual to experience this transformation. It doesn't come from either precision in theology or zealous activism. Christ's Spirit alone gives power and persuasiveness to the endeavors of his followers. Without Christ's presence in an individual's witnessing encounters, the efforts have a hollow ring and are futile.

Apart from this living in Christ's Spirit, several pitfalls develop that either nullify or impede evangelistic decisions. the spiraling cycle of failure in Christian witnessing includes the following characteristics:

First, the believer becomes apathetic in sharing the news of Christ's salvation. The New Testament is basically an account of God's outreach for lost men through the church. Those that committed themselves to Christ in the Gospels and Acts of the apostles had a curious reaction. Once they had encountered the living Christ, and been filled with His Spirit, they enthusiastically sought fellowship with other believers. Their immediate response was to lead others to have a similar experience. It wasn't necessary for them to be prodded or programmed to share their faith. It was a spontaneous reaction.

It is true that the disciples required admonishment to display the fruits of the Spirit. They also needed coaxing to overcome the works of the flesh. But sharing of one's faith in Christ was instinctive and enthusiastic. It was simply the outgrowth of lives in tune with Christ.

William Barclay in *Turning To God*, suggested a variety of elements involved in the converting ministry of the early church. They began by sharing the personal experience of what God had done for them. They provided adequate documentation of the facts of their claims to those persons who listened. Furthermore, they displayed tangible expressions of Christ's love to friends and enemies alike. The ultimate evidence of their faith came in the courageous manner in which they gave up their lives for their savior.

The urgency of evangelism within the church has wavered through twenty centuries. At times it has been like Rip Van Winkle, sleeping through violent revolutions. The spark of Christ's Spirit in faithful disciples has run like a thread in every generation. At times the fire has faded to a flicker, and then it has burned brightly.

Current expressions of apathy toward witnessing inevitably illustrate parallel feelings of unconcern for Christ.

Second, the believer loses perspective of proper priorities in his ministry. There is massive machinery in operation through the organizations of most Christian churches. Quite often there are inadvertent instances in which the institutional organizations take precedence over the central purpose for the machinery's existence.

The church needs a compulsive determination to make Christ known in the lives of desperate persons. But the church inevitably runs the risk of reversing the sequence. It engages in activities without any thought as to the reasons for the programs. Christian social action for the purpose of bringing men to God through Jesus Christ is indispensable to the church. But a social Gospel apart from the foundation ingredient of providing people "wholeness" in God is irrelevance. All the meetings, admirable ministries and planning in the world are unable to serve as substitutes of Christian witnessing. At best, they are expressions of Christian witnessing.

The flip side of activism without purpose is equally destructive. Many churches are content to either continue with weak, lifeless forms of witnessing, or not to witness at all. This again illustrates inverted priorities without a church making vital efforts to bring men into the Kingdom. But this danger is heightened in congregations where there are adequate finances and sufficient persons to occupy the space available on Sunday mornings. Sharing the Gospel with others can too easily be overlooked when the church is too comfortable.

Third, the believer has a limited vision of opportunities to bear witness to Christ. Evangelist Billy Graham provided a prophetic warning at the 1972 Southern Baptist Convention to churches timid about launching bold, innovative ministries to reach unbelievers. The daring, early day evangelistic meetings by Baptists met the rigid opposition of the Established Church because they were different. When the Baptist forefathers shared their faith on the job and with their neighbors, the Established Church viewed it critically. The

Baptist deviation from the formal hymns to Gospel songs was equally controversial. Graham proposed that these daring strides by early Baptists "were attempts to discover powerful, spirit-filled instruments which would express a dynamic faith and which would cause the youth of their generation to respond to the Gospel."[1]

Few contemporary congregations express such boldness! Churches seeking to substitute creative evangelistic efforts for a pattern of feeble Sunday evening participation face stiff opposition. Flexibility in the order of worship, or the use of exciting modern church music, spark additional negative reactions.

Graham concluded that "many Baptist churches have become like a fifteenth century Roman Catholic Church. They really believe that the grace of God comes only through the proper forms — and at the proper times."[2]

A basic element in leading people to a conversion experience in Christ is cultivating sensitive, caring relationships. This ingredient is too often overlooked by those relying exclusively in mass evangelism or the use of memorized formulas to explain salvation. During the nineteenth century, as well as the early twentieth, churches could depend on revival meetings to attract large crowds of unbelieving adults. But the tide had already turned by 1930. Today, with careful and intensive preparation, Billy Graham's meetings will attract unbelieving adults. Few other preachers have this success. Too often, sincere evangelistic preaching is unproductive because only Christians hear it.

Successful evangelism hinges upon unbelievers hearing the Gospel. The church's principle task is to display the love of God by cultivating caring relationships with desperate people through which God can make men whole with His redemptive activity.

Unbelievers generally resist attending worship services. The church's only valid response is to take its message of God's love and redemption into the homes, streets and playgrounds of the community it serves.¹

The church has a dependable tool for the conversion of children called "Sunday School." Donald Metz in a study of suburban churches in *New Congregations* estimated that sixty to eighty percent of a church's new members transfer their membership from another church. He also suggested that baptisms generally occur "as the primaries grow to be juniors."³

The evangelistic effectiveness of Sunday School with children is an exciting bright spot for the church. However, outreach to unchurched adults is comparatively sparse in most churches apart from innovative caring ministries.

Fourth, believers provide too little training in ministering to the needs of desperate people. A midwestern pastor accepted a new church pastorate with a deep obsession for evangelism. He was determined to impress his congregation with the urgency of bringing people to Christ. Week after week he preached on the same theme, "You must win the lost! You must win the lost!"

Several deacons approached the pastor with bewilderment. "We are willing to win the lost, pastor. But when are you going to tell us how to do it?"

Church leaders too often expect evangelistic activity on the part of all believers without first providing adequate training for the task. There is no one way or simple approach that will succeed with every potential convert. The variations in Christian witness are as varied as the needs of the unbeliever.

Pastors and churches have the responsibility of first, properly locating desperate persons with human hurts. They must then devise caring approaches to meet those needs. But the church's task is not complete until it undertakes the responsibility of matching the interests and talents of members with the concerns of troubled persons. The sensitive church will then equip the persons more fully to carry out

PENETRATING BARRIERS OF RESISTANCE

The church is the only institution on earth which can never be content with its progress. The church's mission is incomplete as long as there are people with hurts and Christless hearts in its community and throughout the world. No church can ever be either comfortable or complacent and fulfill her commission from Christ.

Wendell Belew, of the Home Mission Board, stresses the need for boldness and innovation by churches to achieve its basic goal, conversions for Christ. Belew suggested a multiplicity of ways churches can preach Christ in addition to the pulpit, "We need to be open to any avenue for extending the kingdom of God and to seek activities that will help us discover the new doors the Holy Spirit may open."[4]

Belew further conceded his willingness to "put off reaping dividends for a decade if I know we're going to quadruple our investment."[5]

However, most churches with unproductive evangelistic results are unable to supply a valid excuse. Traditional and predictable church programs have been rejected by many communities as both irrelevant and repulsive.

Consider three essential elements in dynamic evangelistic endeavors for the contemporary church congregation:

First, there must be a sensitivity to the desperate needs of people before one can discern the proper godly response. The church's task is to take the message of God's love and redemption into every dimension of our worlds, whether of business and labor or sickness and sorrow. The challenge might include the worlds of politics and poverty or family and children. The church's commission is clearly to take this hope to everyone, everywhere, regardless of their condition. This is the implication of Paul's instruction for Christians to become "all things to all men that by all means, some might be saved." This is Paul's endorsement for the church to make every possible daring expression of love in cultivating men to Christ.

But what happens when the church is adequately sensitive concerning human needs? The congregation that is in resonance with God will create whatever ministries are necessary to meet those needs. God's Spirit will guide the truly caring church to make the proper response.

An increasing number of churches across the nation are utilizing their church buildings daily for a variety of weekday ministries. Day care programs, well-baby clinics and dental clinics are exciting contemporary church ministries. Other congregations have launched literacy and craft classes, recreation programs and a host of similar activities and services. Sensitive churches have added staff members to assist a multitude of volunteers in caring for the personal needs of the congregation and individuals not yet touched by the church.

But many expressions of human compassion will not occur in or around the church building. Many contemporary conversions result from ministries in the streets and homes of desperate people. William Barclay noted that fact in *Turning To God*:

> It is the strange and odd fact that as things now are it is not in the church that we expect to find conversions happening. We have actually come to a state of things when we expect to find conversions happening at missions and campaigns outside the church rather than within the ordinary work, ministry and activity of the church.[6]

There is another element in dynamic evangelism that is as urgent as discovering broken lives to whom the church can minister. That involves acting boldly upon one's discovery.

Second, there must be an expression of courageous faith to follow God's leadership, once it's known. A wave of terms have been used to describe the innovative ministries being utilized by many creative congregations. Some refer to it as "Pre-Evangelism." It has also been called "Saturation Evangelism" and "Unconventional Evangelism." "Cultivative Evangelism" is another exciting and valid description.

Whichever reference one chooses, it denotes a bold determination to bring men to God through Jesus Christ. The blending of one's prayerful concern and bold experimentation in ministry are inevitably used by God to produce converts and bring about church growth.

Church growth is never coincidental. It doesn't just happen anywhere. It isn't the result of someone just stumbling upon responsive people and reaping an instant revival. It involves committed Christians who are suitably dependent on God. It further requires the unrelenting effort to apply Christ's love to those who have never known it.

Timid churches will reject such caring ministries because they are unwilling to pay the price, even though God's will is clear in the matter.

Jesus gave his disciples in all generations a beautiful model for obedience prior to his arrest. He labored with a pail of water and a simple towel to reinforce the appropriate nature of the church as a "servant people."

The implications of a church with courageously innovative ministries are devastating. Buckner Fanning, pastor of the prominent Trinity Baptist Church in San Antonio, Texas posed a sobering series of questions to a meeting of Southern Baptist pastors in 1967,

"What would happen if we took the towel of genuine humility and washed the dirty feet of a tired world? What would happen if we became the 'servants' instead of the 'served'? I believe a God-breathed spirit of renewal would sweep through the very life of Southern Baptists and we would become what many think we already are — the people of God."[7]

Third, the effective witness for Christ needs a life which overflows with the "fruits of the Spirit." An individual must truly have his life possessed with the Holy Spirit, before he will exhibit the "fruits of the Spirit" as Paul listed them in Galatians 5:22. These nine characteristics in a believer's life give authenticity to his life and witness. Few unbelievers express a spontaneous eagerness to discover what they must do to be saved. But the Christian whose life is characterized by love, joy, peace, patience, kindness, goodness, faithfulness, gentleness, and self-control finds the task easier. The unconscious display of such characteristics in a believer's life earns him the right to share his faith to a more responsive audience.

John Wesley, George Whitefield were and Billy Graham is profoundly successful in influencing people to commit their lives to God through Jesus Christ. The words in printed copies of their sermons fail to explain their effectiveness in evangelism. Other men preaching the same words have not seen similar results. The traits of the Holy Spirit within their lives gave evidence that God had empowered them. Each was sensitive and alert to God.

The Spirit of God has been planted on every church field across the nation. In many of these places, there are not yet visible results of God's activity among the populace.

Jesus' prayer life explains the intensity of his obedience to the Father. Through prayer his sensitivity to God was developed to the fullest. This complete sensitivity to God's will explains the success of his redemptive mission. Christ was totally in tune with the Spirit of the Father. When the disciples had unsuccessfully fished all night, Christ instructed them to cast their nets in another place for results. The contemporary disciple who is sensitive to Christ and casts his net of ministry in the places his Lord directs, will see men won to the Kingdom.

The components known as the "fruit of the Spirit" makes up a prism of love in action. I had the privilege of serving as Area Superintendent of Missions in Nebraska with men who exemplified each of the characteristics Paul described. God's love was able to shine through the transparency of their lives and bring others to himself.

Love. Duane McCormick is pastor of the Omaha Baptist Center. He also serves as chaplain for the Douglas County jail system. A member of the Center called Duane's attention to a curious ad in the classified section of the paper, "Lonely man wants a friend." Members at the Center invited the man to visit their services. He came to church the next Sunday in a drunken state.

Duane had compassion for this desperate man and showed special interest in him. He frequently had to track the man down in bars. But Duane's unbreakable goodwill was persistent. The man finally made a commitment to Christ and gradually overcame his alcoholism. Instead of wasting his money on liquor, he began saving money for rent. As the man grew in Christ, he later visited the bars to witness to his old friends.

Duane's compassionate love had been used by God to help transform a worthless drunk into an effective witness for Jesus Christ.

Joy. C.O. Haile formerly pastored the Egan Park Baptist Church in McCook, Nebraska. The congregation was small and it was necessary for him to supplement his income as Director of the Training Center for the Mentally Retarded. C.O.'s life is characterized by joy and it becomes contagious to those who are around him.

Through his secular work he met a 23-year-old retarded man. The young man was overwhelmed by the pastor's joy and concern for him. The pastor's compassionate interest in the man drew him to Christ and the church. Though limited in many ways, the man was able to make a meaningful decision for Christ.

The young man had been seeing a psychiatrist for a long time who did not believe in God. But after the man's conversion, the psychiatrist told the pastor, "That young man's had an experience with the Lord — he's different now."

Peace. Dewey Hickey formerly served as missionary pastor to the First Baptist Church in Valentine, Nebraska. He learned of a sandhill rancher 100 miles from his church who needed a minister. Dewey visited the man in a filthy farmhouse, and found the man was separated from his wife. He noted that the man was currently living with his wife's sister.

Dewey invited the man to talk with him privately in his car. Dewey was at peace with God in the awareness that he must bear a witness to the desperate man. He asked the man if he was "saved," and the man had never heard the term. Still with an inner peace as a stabilizing force, Dewey tried every approach he knew to lead the man to trust Christ and repent of his sins.

In the midst of his confident peace with God, Dewey became alert to what really mattered most to the man. He asked, "Wouldn't you like to have your wife and children back?" The man suddenly became tearful... He put his head in his hands, as if in agony. He abruptly screamed at the top of his lungs, "If what you're talking about can straighten me out so I can get them back, let's do it right now."

The man accepted Christ in the car. Minutes later he proved the sincerity of his decision by asking his wife's sister to leave the farm. He was later reconciled with his wife and children, and became a careful student of the Bible.

God had spoken to Dewey in the midst of his inner peace to remain confident and not allow the initial obstacles to deter him.

Patience. Bill Tritten serves as pastor of the Bethel Baptist Church in Scottsbluff. He was impressed by a woman and her daughters who were active members of his church. However, he was concerned for the husband who was unconverted.

Bill visited the husband on his ranch, but discovered the man had little interest in talking about the things of God. He soon found that his best opportunity to talk with the man was at the corral, while the rancher tried to break his wild horses.

Bill didn't care much for horses. But it was apparent that the rancher's life centered about horses. Over a period of months Bill patiently learned to ride horseback in order to establish his trustworthiness with the rancher.

Bill continued visiting for over a year before the man made his decision to trust Christ as his saviour. Bill's persistent, patient concern had penetrated the man's resistence to Christ.

Kindness. Bob Mustian served as pastor of the Trinity Baptist Church in Benkleman, Nebraska and supplemented his income by working in a grocery store. After moving to the church he learned of a family who hadn't attended church in five years. He discovered that the teenage son was crippled and retarded. The church people had immediate concern and looked for every opportunity to express kindness in a tangible way. Bob decided that every day on his way to the grocery store he would take the youth to school. The boy had previously been a drop-out. Bob drove by, lifted the heavy youth in his arms and carried him to the car. Upon arriving at school, he repeated the process.

The family was deeply moved by the pastor's care for their son. Within a year the boy's two younger sisters trusted Christ as savior, and the parents returned to regular church attendance.

Goodness. Frank Miller is the pastor of the York Baptist Church in the eastern part of the state. Frank serves as a civil employee in addition to pastoring the congregation. He learned that a couple who lived over 20 miles away was interested in the church. The pastor expressed the goodness of his heart by driving that distance four times every Sunday to pick them up and take them home again. Mrs. Miller provided meals for these people who were without any means of transportation.

After the couple had experienced the goodness of the pastor and his wife for several months, Christ became real in their lives. The woman accepted Christ as her Lord and was baptized into the church fellowship.

Faithfulness. Irvin Burlison has pastored the Immanuel Baptist Church in Grand Island, Nebraska since 1960. Several years ago Irvin counseled with a young couple who were interested in the church. The woman had not come from an evangelical background and had been baptized as a baby. The pastor was determined to remain faithful to the Biblical teachings on baptism and confront the couple with this truth.

The pastor asked the young woman why she had chosen to be baptized. The young woman was shocked by the impact of the pastor's words, and said that she hadn't "chosen" to be baptized.

Remaining faithful to the Scriptures, Irvin answered, "You mean you've never made a decision for Christ on your own? How unfortunate! Everyone ought to have the chance for such a choice." She agreed and made a decision for Christ.

Gentleness. Joe Conaway is the pastor of the Calvary Baptist Church in Sidney, Nebraska. During the early years of his ministry there, he had secular employment as an ambulance drive for a funeral home.

One summer day he was called to the scene of an accident with his ambulance. A twelve-year-old child had been hit and killed by a car. Joe picked up the dead body and carried it to the ambulance. The pastor met the boy's heartbroken family, and saw the need for an expression of gentleness. The pastor and a caring layman, who was a local policeman, visited the boy's family. They expressed a gentle concern for other children in the family. When the family discovered the pastor had been the first to find the boy after the accident, they felt closely drawn to him.

The entire family had since made commitments to Christ and come into the church fellowship. Through an unexpected occasion of crises, Joe had expressed gentleness, and ultimately cultivated a family for Christ.

Self-Control. Henry Wambolt started several mission churches in Nebraska. During his pastorate in Chappell, he ministered to a congregation of about 25 members, and served in a secular job with an electrical plant. Henry was quite responsive when he learned that a new couple in the community had an interest in the Baptist church. He observed that the wife was a professing Christian, but the husband was not. Over a period of months the pastor established a friendship with the couple. But the husband refused to talk to the pastor about spiritual matters. Henry was tempted to give up, and seek more responsive prospects for his church.

But God gave Henry an adequate self-control to deal with the situation. Henry realized that the man was timid to discuss his faith in his wife's presence. Henry's patient self-control proved beneficial.

One day he drew the man out to the car for a private conversation. Here in this setting, the man would not have to be embarrassed about a humble submission to Christ in his wife's presence. Henry invited the man to make the decision for Christ, and he agreed. Within two weeks the man and six other members of his family were baptized.

Even after every possible approach seemed futile, God used Henry's self-discipline to transform the lives of a man and six children.

ONE-TO-ONE, PERSON-TO-PERSON ENCOUNTERS

Everyone longs at one time or another for someone to listen to their problems. Too few turn to their parents for fear of bringing them sorrow. Too few friends seem to have the wisdom to counsel wisely. It is generally impossible for one's mate to be adequately objective or impartial for perfect guidance. Many are too fearful of condemnation to turn to a pastor. Even God seems too far away for multitudes of people to trust. People therefore search for someone who is a combination of parent, friend, mate, pastor and God.

Countless persons are searching for someone who really cares for them. They are in quest of sincere understanding and acceptance. They are confident that with proper support and encouragement they'll be able to grind through their circumstances in their own way.

TELEPHONE

Counseling Desperate people across the nation have found comfort and human compassion from a caring voice over a telephone line. Several thousand hotlines or telephone counseling services have developed since the mid 1960's in America.

Several years ago the Marble Collegiate Church of New York initiated a telephone counseling service. There were 2,743 persons who called for help in the first week. The requests ranged from 354 who needed to find an apartment, to twelve threatening suicide.

Southern Baptists initiated a telephone counseling pilot project in Philadelphia in 1969. A caption in the personal column of the classified ads read, "If you have emotional or spiritual problems and don't know where to turn for help, call H04-9708 between 10 and 4 Friday for Minister's Counsel." Several million people read the notice in the three daily Philadelphia papers.

One of the most avid searchers was a lady from one of the newspapers who called each week to renew the ad. She would then seek help in her search for God and agony over personal problems for 30 minutes to an hour.

Almost half of the callers spoke of personal problems, while one-third worried about marital crises. Others had parent-child conflicts and religious problems.

The callers ranged from 10 to 80 years, with more than half being between 20-40. More than a third were Catholic, with nearly that number being Protestant. While one of seven Philadelphians is Jewish, only one of 20 callers were Jewish.

During the nine month experimental ministry, there were 20 to 25 calls per day. Some conversations lasted over an hour, while others talked for only several minutes.

Three of every four callers were housewives. Working men and women called, saying they'd need to call back later.

The ministry was successful because callers could remain anonymous. Some made confessions that they'd never told to another person.

Some callers had a primary need to talk with someone who cared. Others with deep-seeded problems were referred to psychiatrists, physicians or social workers.

In five years of ministry in the "City of Brotherly Love," in my opinion few services provided by Southern Baptists so dramatically reached and helped the masses of troubled people in the area.

The Benson Presbyterian Church in suburban Omaha, Nebraska provided facilities for a similar ministry. The church cooperates in a telephone hotline ministry, known as Sunshine Rescue Service. Their motto was "You Don't Have To Crash Alone." This youth assistance agency offered counseling or extended rap sessions for troubled persons. Many callers begin by being anonymous, and later come in for in-person confrontations.

American Baptists in Los Angeles provided counseling assistance, known as HELP. More than 800 persons per month are referred to churches and agencies at this number.

The St. Stephens Episcopal Church in Milburn, N.J., sponsored a Dial-A-Friend service. Distraught people could make contact with a helpful person.

In Davenport, Iowa, there was a Dial-A-Listener service.

This service was state supported, as it was offered by the Iowa State Commission on Aging. It was geared to the needs of lonely senior citizens. A survey in the area revealed that loneliness was the principal problem of the elderly. Finances, housing and illness were other troublesome problems on the list.

Quite often teens called the number. This led to the acquisition of funds to establish a youth hotline with four telephones for operation between 8 p.m. and midnight.

Crises Center: The Worcester Church has cooperated with the Jaycee organization to deal with community drug abuse. A Crises Center was established in the basement of the church. The idea behind it was to involve people in helping people in an accepting, anonymous, and non-judgmental way. The Crises Center was established to satisfy a need in the community through the concern, skills, and understandings of its staff, and by referring people to the individuals in the community who were best able to cope with the clients' problems.

The Jaycees provided the training sessions and paid for phones, postage and coffee for the staff.

The staff of the Crises Center consists mainly of college students and persons under 25 years. The Crises Center referred people to 54 separate agencies in the area.

In a six month sample period 1,748 calls were received.

Included were 115 youth drug problems among the young, (82 were heroin), 74 runaways, 44 medical problems, 55 job counseling problems, 29 suicide potentials, 10 veneral disease problems and 8 homosexuals.

Follow-Up To Television Broadcast: The North Phoenix Baptist Church of Phoenix, Arizona, experienced significant church growth with a telephone ministry.

The church televised their Sunday worship services live into three states. During the first five minutes of the service a pre-recorded special appeal was made to the TV audience as the church's telephone number was imposed on the screen.

At noon each Sunday four men sat waiting for the phones to ring. A great number of the callers eventually attended the services. Many calls came from people seeking salvation, comfort, or prayer. Other frequent calls came from patients in the hospital.

In a two year period, 25 percent of the church's new members came as a result of the broadcast. Many of the people made their first step by phone.

Telephone Survey: "Telephone evangelism" is the name that the Thomas Road Baptist Church of Lynchburg, Va., gives to its telephone ministry. The pastor asked 109 persons to come forward during prayer meeting. Each one was given a page from the telephone directory. The volunteers were also supplied with a mimeographed greeting to use in asking people to attend Sunday School.

The SBC Home Mission Board has prepared a manual for telephone surveys. It is the Urban Church Survey Manual. In several minutes a caller is able to obtain any necessary information he desires for the church records. The telephone survey is as effective as a door-to-door sampling, and three times faster. Callers are encouraged to avoid the professional and canned approach of a telephone magazine salesman. Informality and sincerity are the key ingredients of the successful telephone survey. A telephone visitor can make about 201 cultivative calls in two hours.

The Frankford Avenue Baptist Church in the Kensington section of Philadelphia had satisfying results from the survey. The congregation utilized the survey when they had less than 30 members. A criss-cross telephone directory was rented from a subsidiary of the telephone company, listing the telephone number of every house on every street in order.

Several thousand calls helped locate hundreds of unchurched persons who were interested in the church's ministries. Twenty percent of the calls at one point were with possible church prospects. The overall average of calls that turned up prospects was one out of every eight persons.

The Baptist survey manual is most valuable for the six follow-up letters and the suggested telephone cultivation visits.

The final letter, which is the culmination of some dozen mailing and telephone contacts to build bridges of friendship is the request for a personal appointment. This sixth letter informs the family that a visitor wants to present them with the gift of a marked New Testament in their home.

When the actual presentation of the Bible is made, the atmosphere should be fertile enough for a personal presentation of God's salvation.

The criss-cross directory is generally the most acceptable source of names and numbers. However, 19 other sources of names and addresses of newcomers include: chamber of commerce, city hall, welcome wagon, newcomer service, the person who takes water, electricity, telephones, and gas service orders, the man who connects water, electricity, telephones and gas meters, the postman, real estate salesmen, moving companies, mortgage companies and lending agencies, apartment managers, managers of trailer parks and personnel managers of large companies.

As a result of the survey in Philadelphia, the church had an increase of membership by 20 percent with the telephone survey and six month follow-up process.

Prayer Service: Many churches have a "dial-a-prayer" ministry. One First Baptist Church initiated a "live" prayer ministry with additional church telephones over five years ago.

Initially, a special committee was appointed to explore the ministry. According to the pastor, church recommendations included: "(1) A special telephone installed solely for this purpose. (2) Specific hours when people might be invited to call. (3) The availability of the pastor when possible, and the use of staff members, deacons, or others whom the pastor might select when he was unavailable. (4) The ministry be publicized through the newspapers, the church paper, the church bulletin, announcements over our weekly radio program..."[1]

The largest number of callers per day was 14. On some occasions no one called. Persons who were sick or had sick friends called. People with family troubles called. Alcoholics, and people facing difficult decisions or tasks requested prayer.

Recorded Devotionals: The Belmont Heights Baptist Church of Nashville began an "Instant Inspiration" ministry in 1966. This means of communication allows the opportunity for Bible centered devotionals, as well as announcements of revival services and special events.

The following procedure helped the church develop a listing audience: "(1) Secure a telephone number that is easy to remember. (2) Use someone with a pleasing telephone voice. (3) Use the question method to interest people in calling your number. "Are you lonely?" (4) Be positive in your approach. (5) Be sympathetic and understanding in your approach."[2]

Advertising on restaurant coffee coasters or business cards and telephone stickers are additional methods of promoting the ministries. Notices in the hotel church directory and chamber of commerce guide can assist with publicity.

Referrals: The "Granddaddy" of the telephone counseling

or referral services is FISH. The symbol of Christian commitment in ancient times was the fish. The service of ministering to the distressed in the name of FISH began at St. Andrews' Church Old Headington Oxford, England. It began because there was "the need of an organization ready to help on short notice. . .(and) a way of fulfilling the Lord's commandment to love our neighbor."[3]

In the United States Robert Lee Howell adapted this concept for an Episcopal initiated lay ministry in 1964. Howell began it when he was rector of the Church of the Good Shepherd in West Springfield, Massachusetts, saying,

"I have adapted the Fish at St. Andrews into a plan which I believe would be workable in West Springfield. A commercial telephone answering service, on duty twenty-four hours a day, seven days a week, and answering for the Fish would be our point of contact with the person needing help."[4]

Rev. Howell gave the ministry its initial promotion with teenagers delivering handbills to over 7,000 homes. Information about FISH appears in a monthly edition of the *International* at one dollar for a year's subscription. The address is Box 697, Hillsboro, Texas 76645.

There are now more than 2000 FISH groups functioning in the United States. Thirty-six groups have begun in the Chicago area alone.

PERSONAL SERVICES

Medical

Well Baby Clinics: The Ervay Street Baptist Center of Dallas, Texas initiated an immunization clinic and well-baby clinic. In the beginning pastor-director J.D. Holt asked, "What type of clinic do we need? Do we need a baby clinic, a sick clinic, a dental clinic, an immunization clinic, or do we need a family counseling clinic?"[5]

Rev. Holt and his survey committee talked to doctors, City-County Health Department officials and community people. It was decided to have a nurse at the clinic to talk with mothers about their children's health. The pastor realized that public school nurses, doctors and public health officials can give assistance in discovering community health problems.

The First Baptist Church of Mt. Pleasant, S.C. provided a well-baby clinic for residents of the community. Two physicians and three nurses examine and give shots to as many as fifty children a day.

Medical Clinic: Rev. Dan Grubb is pastor-director of the Penrose Baptist Chapel-Center in a low income community of South Philadelphia. He realized that the residents in his community were not receiving adequate medical attention.

He made arrangements with two physicians to provide a room in his storefront church building to the doctors for a small rental arrangement. Two or three nights per week the physicians treat numerous sick residents of the neighboring government housing project. The pastor often lingers among the people in the waiting room to cultivate friendships. Tracts with inspirational messages are provided for those persons awaiting treatment.

The chapel sees this medical service as a part of its overall ministry in Christ's name.

The Second Baptist Church of Little Rock, Arkansas has a diversity of ministries to human need. Dr. Dale Cowling says, "We believe we must begin to preach the gospel at the point of the individual's needs."[6] The church has therefore established a medical clinic for the poor. Some women in the church have volunteered for service as highly professional nursing technicians and nutritionists.

In October, 1969, the church began a medical clinic in the McKay section of Little Rock, Arkansas, where 6,000 low income people live. Dr. Jasper McPhail, a church member, has about forty patients in his clinic on a typical Tuesday and Thursday night. A professional nutritionist counsels obese and diabetic patients.

Cooperation with Community Health Agencies: The First Baptist Church of Eagle Butte, South Dakota, cooperates with the Public Health Hospital (Indian). The women of the church provide layettes for the new babies.

Rev. J.M. Oswalt, pastor of the First Baptist Church of Hammond, Louisiana, has led his church to a number of helping ministries. The church cooperates with the Public Health and Public Welfare agencies in providing assistance for destitute persons and families.

The Little River Baptist Church of Miami, Florida, discovered a great need for a medical clinic. It implemented the ministry in cooperation with the Dade County Medical Association.

The Detroit Baptist Association built a Baptist center near the section that was destroyed in the riots of 1967. One of the first projects on the drawing board for the center's ministry was a well-baby clinic. Plans were made to work with the local health department and local physicians in an outpatient effort for babies and small children.

Planned Parenthood Clinics: The Oklahoma City Baptist Center began providing a Planned Parenthood Clinic in 1965 as one of about twenty activities geared to combat the difficulties of its deprived community. Some 350 young people came for assistance in a one year period.

The Planned Parenthood Association of Oklahoma County in conjunction with the Oklahoma Medical Association and Community Chest provided the operation and personnel for this ministry. The Baptist Center provided the meeting space and patients.

A nurse and gynecologist staffed the clinic for three hours each Friday. The center directors, Rev. and Mrs. John V.

Hawk, saw the ministry as a help in fulfilling the Center's philosophy: "The Whole Gospel for the Whole Need of the Whole Person."[7]

Rev. Hawk said, "I feel that this (planned parenthood) is not only entirely compatible with the will of God but also in keeping with the responsibility that God expects his children to exercise in this matter of providing for one's family."[8]

Hawk realized that any useful information could be used to further evil as well as good. He said he had an unrealized ambition to cultivate very definite individual and personal relationships with everyone who was enrolled in his programs. The diverse ministries enabled him to win and baptize as many as 44 persons in one year.

Local churches could provide a similar ministry by inviting a physician and nurse from the public health department to speak on the subject to young wives. The church can contact Planned Parenthood, 515 Madison Avenue, New York, N.Y. 10022. Planned Parenthood has a national registry of physicians, hospitals and clinics.

Food Distribution

Rev. Jack Hyles is pastor of the First Baptist Church of Hammond, Indiana, the church with the largest Sunday School in the nation. Hyles testifies that his church "out-socializes the social-action liberals." He refers to the free hot meals that the church distributes to the poor each week. The church also gives away clothes, baskets of food and money to persons in need. Hyles states that his church "does more social action on the way to reach sinners than any liberal church in America."

"Meals-On-Wheels" is a food distribution program throughout the country. In many places the local Jaycee organization enlists five churches, each to assume the preparation and delivery of food one day per week. The Trinity Baptist Church in Benkleman, Nebraska, has less than fifty active members. Former pastor, Rev. James Tolbert and his predecessor Rev. Bob Mustian both participated in the ministry to the disabled in the community of 1,500 people.

The Wake Forest Baptist Church in Winston-Salem, N.C., began sponsoring the Meals on Wheels program in September, 1962. They discovered people in the community who couldn't have nutritionally balanced diets. The elderly, handicapped, convalescents and others who weren't able to prepare meals or go out for them needed help.

The Wake Forest Baptist Church leadership consulted with the mayor's commission for a model community. A plan was developed in which the church and the North Carolina Baptist Hospital would cooperate in the project. A trained nutritionist at the hospital prepares the meals, and the church volunteers deliver them.

Each day Monday through Friday two meals are provided in the form of a hot lunch and cold supper. Over 9,000 meals were taken to the homes of both blacks and whites who are either elderly or handicapped. Meals are provided at the cost of only $1.25 per day or $6.25 per week. The delivery man on Monday collects for the week's deliveries. The Department of Public Welfare pays seventy cents a day for the bill of clients they recommend.

Eight other churches now participate to ease the burden for the Wake Forest Baptist Church.

The Richmond, Virginia Council of Women's Organizations also sponsors a Meals-On-Wheels service.

The First Baptist Church of Washington, D.C., is cooperating with the New York Avenue Presbyterian Church in a Meals-on-Wheels effort. Volunteers from the Baptist Diaconate are providing meals for elderly and shut-in persons. The Presbyterian Church prepares the meal and coordinates deliveries.

The Baptist volunteers deliver the prepared hot meals to the recipients. A driver and helper are utilized in each car.

Visitors stay long enough to greet the client, place the food on the table, and pick up containers from the previous day. There is a nominal fee for the service to defray food cost.

Dwayne Zimmer of the Bayshore Baptist Church in Tampa, Florida says, "Any church or group of churches with enough concern and a strong enough desire to begin and continue such a service may do so if they can find a restaurant, hospital or catering service willing to prepare the meals."[9] The ministry provides opportunities for Bible study and Christian witness.

Housing

Youth Facility: The Highland Avenue Baptist Church of Queens, New York, has acquired an apartment building on property near their church to house young adults. The Youth Hostel offers the church the chance to minister to transients, and care for transplanted Baptist youth. This church facility builds bridges of friendship with unchurched youth and helps the church relate them to Christ. The housing ministry is self-supporting from modest rental fees.

The Lincoln Park Baptist Church in San Francisco rents part of a house to hippie youth near Haights Street. The church works through the United Youth ministries directed by Kent Philpott. A seminary student leads a Bible study dialogue three nights a week and several hippies have become Christians.

Family Provisions: The Metropolitan New York Baptist Association is cooperating in a project called T.O.N.E. A non-profit corporation of Christian people provides apartments in Harlem for anxious tenants. Dr. Cal Guy served as interim Missions Director of the association when the plans were initiated.

Rev. Rodolph Morgan, the black pastor who heads the effort says, "The people come from pathetic surroundings and living conditions. You have to show them by actions that you care about them. That's why we started T.O.N.E. Landlords don't repair plumbing. When people complain, the housing authority requires landlords to lower rent. Landlords can't make any profit, so they give up the property. That's where we stepped in with Southern Baptist connections through Dr. Cal Guy."[10]

Some 200 persons are served with new landlords now who treat them right. Pastors provide Bible studies to care for the spiritual needs. They show genuine concern for the total living conditions of the residents. The group hopes to secure another building in which the members of the church might live in an authentic Christian community.

Retirement Accommodations: The Walnut Street Baptist Church of Louisville, Kentucky, has established the Baptist Towers, a multi-storied, 200-unit, high-rise apartment. This facility provided low-cost housing for the elderly.

The First Baptist Church of Longview, Washington, is building a 52-unit retirement home to offer low-cost housing for senior citizens with small incomes. Pastor Ted Curtis reports that a live-in supervisor will lead Bible study and offer transportation for the residents.

Legal

When ministers and Christian laymen establish themselves as trustworthy and reliable friends, youth will approach them concerning legal problems. The charges may range from shoplifting or possession of marijuana, to driving without a license. The more disadvantaged a community, the more probable that a minister will be approached for help.

Rev. Edwin Armitage is director of Youth and Family Services for Southern Baptists in Cincinnati, Ohio. He is engaged in referring youth to legal assistance. Armitage says, "On a given day I am in contact with a number of probation officers, caseworkers, lawyers, policemen, referees, the judge, and probation and parole staff (Ohio Youth Commission)."[11]

Armitage has worked with the Ohio Youth Commission. He helps gain the release of youth who are unable to go back to their own homes by securing them homes.

Rev. J.M. Oswalt of the First Baptist Church, Hammond, Louisiana, has indicated a special legal ministry of his church. They offer a program of marriage counseling, including referrals from three law firms.

The pastor of the Coranado Baptist Chapel in San Diego is a lawyer and Air Force Reserve Colonel. His church is located on a community island where the military base is located. Rev. James Roamer, the pastor, offers his legal services to the military personnel as a ministry. He has moved his ministry to the church so that people might become familiar with it.

Pastor R.D. "Jack" Baker of the First Baptist Church led in the establishment of the Cooperative Church ministries offices in London, Kentucy. Twelve denominations participate in the project. Recently, a lawyer donated time to take a disabled and unemployed man to Lexington for reconsideration of his disability case.

Deep friendships of a pastor and young people are established and enhanced through these efforts. Close-knit ties are cemented with their parents in many cases, also. It provides a natural entree for consideration of a family's spiritual problems.

Educational

Across the nation churches provide a generous diversity of educational ministries to their communities. The most extensive efforts are full-scale school systems for first grade through high school in Baptist churches.

Other churches provide educational helps through grades or specialized educational classes. These ministries will be discussed in Chapter III. Most common and characteristic of the one-to-one, person-to-person encounters are tutoring and literacy.

Tutoring: Several years ago, *Home Missions Magazine* reported that "Each year a quarter of a million of the nation's youth fail to complete elementary school and a million drop out before finishing high school." The seeds of the dropout problem appear to begin early in the elementary years when students first begin to fail in reading. Awareness of this urgent problem has motivated many to respond.

The birth of a tutoring program at First Baptist Church in San Antonio illustrates the evolution of a vital helping ministry. The church's elementary director perceived of the need for tutoring of pupils at a downtown elementary school near the church. The church staff directed her to assume the project in October, 1969.

The principal, faculty and PTA executive committee at Travis Elementary School encouraged the project. The elementary director recruited the initial tutors personally. High school students who were adept in principles of the new math were also enlisted. Church youth were trained in phonics and mathematics in the Sunday night church training period.

Permission slips were distributed to children at school to release the school from liability and to allow the children to ride on church transportation. The first day 250 children arrived for the tutoring. Each tutored child was also able to have refreshments and go skating in the gym during the two hour session. The first three grades now receive tutoring on a different day from the upper three grades because of the large number of students. The children's needs were greatest in mathematics and reading. Therefore, the church concentrated on math and remedial reading in their tutoring provisions.

Children in culturally deprived communities generally enter school two years behind children from middle class homes. Church tutoring programs seek to help the child by increasing "his motivation to learn; let him know someone cares; help him improve school work and reach maximum capabilities;

reinforce skills taught in school; strengthen his ability to cope with himself and his environment; and provide a place to study away from crowded home conditions."[12]

Literacy: Southern Baptist churches have assisted thousands of adults in learning to read through the Laubach method of literacy training. The S.B.C. Women's Missionary Union has equipped numerous women across the nation to teach adults to read.

Mrs. G.W. Bullard, while her husband was Executive Director of the Delaware Valley Baptist Association, taught the pastor of a Polish Baptist congregation to speak and read English. She has led Associational clinics to train others in the skill of literacy instruction.

The former directors of Christian Social Ministries at the Central Nassau Baptist Church on Long Island, N.Y., were Rev. and Mrs. Jerry L. Scruggs. Mrs. Scruggs taught immigrants to read in order that they could become American citizens. A forty year old native of Italy was trained over a six-month's period by Mrs. Scruggs to pass the educational test for naturalization. Today that woman "has her papers and praises God that someone cared enough to teach her to read and write," according to the Associational newsletter.

In Philadelphia's inner city, Brenda Forlines formerly provided individual literacy assistance through the Frankford Avenue Baptist Church weekday ministries. Mothers and fathers of children in her arts and crafts clubs sought her help in reading.

Clothing

One of the most popular and helpful services of Baptist churches for disadvantaged communities is a clothes' closet. The Second Baptist Church of Little Rock, Arkansas, has a vital clothing ministry. Used clothing is sorted, repaired, sized and fitted for the needy.

The Omaha Baptist Center has one day a week for free

clothes distribution. The recipients are generally involved in clubs and other spiritual ministries of the center. Virtually every Southern Baptist Center has a similar clothing ministry, though some have a token charge for the clothing.

In South Dakota, the women of the twenty-two member First Baptist Church of Eagle Butte provide a complete outfit of clothing for newborn Indian infants. The women of First Southern Baptist Church of Great Falls, Montana, have a room stocked with used clothing for emergency use in the community.

Through relationships initiated with a clothing ministry, Christians have earned the right to gain an audience and bear witness for Jesus Christ.

Ministry to Newcomers

The Bluegrass Baptist Church of Hendersonville, Tennessee, has devised a "Welcome-To-Town" project. A church committee secures the names of all newcomers and arranges a visit with them within ten days of their arrival in the city.

Visitors serve as resource persons for information about the community. They seek to complement the service of the Welcome Wagon by providing information the other organization omits. The church representatives take a small gift, such as Good News For Modern Man, and a packet of leisure reading material to every home. General denominational reading matter which is provided includes *Home Life, People* and *Open Windows*. Age group literature for the children is offered: *More* (age 6-7), *Adventure* (8-11) and *Event*.

They also extend an invitation to Bible study. The visitors secure any necessary information about members of the family for the church staff. The visitor attempts to discover the needs and interests of family members, and be a resource person to help meet those needs.

The First Baptist Church of Charleston, S.C., has a unique ministry for newcomers that includes a bus tour of historic landmarks in the city. This ministry will be discussed under the section concerning bus ministries.

Family Ministries

Big Brothers — Big Sisters: Countless urban families have only one parent. The Big Brothers civic organization has sought to help boys without a father have an even chance in life. Concerned men select a fatherless boy through the organization, for whom they give special attention.

In Omaha, Nebraska, the YWCA has begun a "Big Sister" program for lonely and neglected girls.

A national consultation on the mission of the suburban church was held in October, 1971, by the Southern Baptist Home Mission Board. One study group on "Forms of Mission and Ministry in Suburbia" recommended a "Big Brother/Sister" program. Suggestions were made that the church train persons to assist social-care agencies in service to underprivileged or delinquent children.

Southern Baptist churches have devised similar ministries to operate through their churches for troubled children. Judith Ann Bair, while director of Christian Social Ministries at the Metropolitan Baptist Church of Cambridge, Mass. began a "Big Sister" program for neglected girls on probation from youth court.

Edwin I. Armitage provides the equivalent of "Big Brothers and Big Sisters" ministry in Cincinnati for community youth. He assigns sponsors for children needing and wanting special counsel and friendship with a Christian adult.

Babysitting: Church ministries are ideally devised to meet some human need in the name of Christ. One urgent need that Baptist leaders have detected with great frequency is the frustrated mother who needs to get out of a houseful of small children. Churches in many areas have selected similar solutions.

The Temple Baptist Church of Champaign, Illinois,

initiated a program to assist and relieve these mothers. Pastor J.P. Bright says, "Recognizing that mothers of preschoolers need an opportunity to have some time alone, ladies in our congregation developed a Mother's Morning Out on Wednesday Mornings."[3] Regular paid staff and rotating volunteers provide care and planned activities for one dollar per child from 9:00-11:30 a.m. The program is licensed by the state and used mostly by mothers who aren't members.

Rev. Bob W. Brackney, Director of Christian Social Ministries for Keystone Baptist Association (Pa.) assists churches in setting up a similar day care activity under a variety of names — Mother's Day Off or Drop-Off ministry. By whatever name, the service has the potential for establishing strong ties between the churches and participating families.

Both the Highland Avenue Baptist Church of Long Island and its mission, Utopia Parkway Baptist Church, have utilized a weekday "drop-off program" for mothers with great success. This ministry is one of a series of ministries that has produced dramatic church growth at Highland Avenue Church.

Vocational

The Little River Baptist Church in Miami, Florida, has an intensive selection of ministries to its local community. The church discovered that a large number of people had problems in securing jobs.

In its efforts to meet this great need, the church began a job placement service as one of its ministries to the community. This helping relationship has opened doors for spiritual assistance.

The Canon of the Church of England, Bryan Green, spoke of the process of conversion as having three stages — pre-evangelism, evangelism and pastoral work. In his book, *The*

Practice of Evangelism, which was written in 1951, he wrote, "By pre-evangelism, I mean the breaking down of the walls which separate the Church from the people outside, the making of contacts between Christians and the world, the taking of the things of God and interpreting them to those who need to know."[14]

The one-to-one, person-to-person ministries in this chapter would qualify as types of pre-evangelism. Any or all of them, under the leadership of God's Spirit may prepare hardened or indifferent hearts for conversion to Christ.

SMALL GROUP APPROACHES

Great things can happen in small groups. The Methodist Church began as a small group church in England. In recent years there has been a resurgence of these gatherings for the renewal of faith among Christian people. This chapter will present a variety of small groups with the intention of initiating friendship for Christ's sake.

There are instances in which the assistance of a single individual is not adequate to meet some personal problem. The presence of a group of concerned friends in a Christian atmosphere may more adequately solve the individual's dilemma. People may draw strength from the intensive interpersonal relations with others.

The group may consist of instructional or caring helps and lessons known as classes. Similarly, the assistance may be expressed as a church provides meaningful, social experiences for one's free time.

Classes

At least nine main types of categories are being practiced throughout the nation with success.

Household Hints

Homemaking Demonstrations: Miss Helen Neiger, while formerly serving as Director of Community ministries at Worcester Baptist Chapel, would take ladies in the community to a home demonstration at a General Foods kitchen. The ladies were taught and allowed to cook there. Miss Neiger has suggested that contacts with Public Health Departments in many large communities would afford such an opportunity.

Nutrition: Mrs. Don Weeks of the Gary Baptist Church,

Gary, Indiana, offers a nutrition class at the church. The ladies are taught to make such food as banana bread. In addition to cooking helps, Mrs. Weeks also assists ladies in the class in buying groceries and planning meals.

A professional nutritionist counsels obese and diabetic patients at the Baptist medical clinic in McKay, Arkansas (within Little Rock).

Certain foods are obviously more nutritional than others. A teacher may emphasize the four basic food groups necessary for adults and children. Free educational literature on family nutrition and health is available from: Metropolitan Life Insurance Company, Health and Welfare Division, 1 Madison Avenue, New York, N.Y. 10010.

Cooking: Churches with seldom used kitchen facilities have found a cooking class a means of good building stewardship. In smaller churches the women can divide into small groups and go to homes. Both demonstrations and supervised cooking are needed items. Helpful recipes of staple food like beans, potatoes and rice are useful.

Foreign missionaries provide a similar ministry of outreach. In Africa, Miss Estelle Freeland directs weekday programs at the Baptist Church in Abidjan, capital of the Ivory Coast. She teaches women in her cooking class some dishes they can prepare on charcoal burners on the ground. She also uses a two-burner gas stove on a table to teach the native women the convenience of a table.

Money Management: Pastor Isidoro Garza of the Second Spanish Baptist Church of San Francisco has opened the church buildings for community service programs. The church provides a disadvantaged person the chance to learn economic buying techniques in a class study. This and other services have given the church numerous opportunities for a ministry to individuals and families. The pastor says, "We have shown the community that we care."[1]

Grooming: A class in grooming may express the necessary

care and concern to earn an opportunity to witness to a teenage girl. Results have been successful from California to Pennsylvania.

Rev. Sid Smith operates the Baptist-sponsored House of Agape in Los Angeles for the girl parolees that are in its care. A class in grooming is led by an attractive black girl who is also a parolee. She cultivates a class of four or five girls at a time. This ministry has successfully reached girls for Christ and the church, according to California Baptist Missions' Director, Ralph Longshore.

The Valley Baptist Church in Conyngham, Pennsylvania, began a class in 1970, known as "Charm 70." The pastor's wife, Mrs. June Craig, wanted to help the girls attending the church. The charm and hygiene course enlisted sixty-two girls with another fifty-two on the waiting list.

Merchants in the community donated hygiene and cosmetic articles. Professional people gave their free time. The pastor's wife was soon leading a community wide project. Several youths were won to Christ through this effort. A similar course was developed for the girls' parents.

The Graceland Baptist Church of New Albany, Indiana, began a beauty club for girls in 1968. For six weeks, beauticians who were members of the church taught the girls how to do their hair and nails. This developed into a program of beauty studies such as modeling, dramatics and Bible study. If the need exists, local churches might have effective ministries using this approach. The possibilities are quite diverse. A visiting beautician could use the basic principles of hair styling on a single girl for demonstration. A dermatologist may speak on skin care. Posture and weight reducing methods might also be used. Discussion on current clothing styles could be another area of general interest.

Sewing: Miss Brenda Forlines utilized a sewing class at Philadelphia's inner-city, Frankford Avenue Baptist Church. She used funds in her weekday ministry budget to purchase the machines. Skilled community ladies assisted by teaching local unchurched housewives to sew.

There is also a sewing class at the 3,300 member Wieuca Road Baptist Church in Atlanta. The group stitches up clothes for the Baptist Mission Center distribution. The ladies also sew for needy persons they discover through other church ministries.

Miss Estelle Freeland of the Baptist Church in Abidjan, provides three sewing classes in the Mossi settlement in Africa. A young Yoruba tailor teaches one, while Miss Freeland teaches two more at suburban Marcory and at Koumassi. Two of the women who attend class at Koumassi have made professions of faith in Christ.

Young women from the Oakwood Baptist and First Baptist Churches, in Lubbock, Texas, began sewing classes in a predominantly Spanish area where there is a Baptist church.

An experienced seamstress teaches the class twice a week. In addition to learning to sew, the women meet for fellowship and the sharing of Christian experiences. Devotionals, in Spanish, are led by the co-pastor. Additional volunteers mend clothes for the clothing room.

A sewing class is strategic because it gives a woman a chance to create something that will help her family. Sewing is best taught through personal instruction with about two pupils per teacher.

Health

Previous consideration has been given to the church's personal expressions of concern and service for the individual's physical health needs.

There are notable illustrations of classes related to helping overweight persons and those addicted to alcohol and drugs. Other classes geared to therapy for mental and emotional problems, serve effectively for church outreach.

Exercise: An exercise class may appeal to persons who are

either overweight or those who want to maintain good physical condition. The Nineteenth Avenue Baptist Church of San Francisco sponsors such a class in a high-density population area.

The pastor's wife leads a Tuesday morning exercise class for women. She then leads a Bible study at the conclusion of the class.

Alcohol Treatment Classes

Alcohol Anonymous Group: Wayne Oates says, "Alcoholics Anonymous is an informal fellowship of men and women who have admitted to themselves that they are powerless to deal with alcohol and have joined themselves together to ask divine aid and help one another as a fellowship of sufferers."[2]

The Temple Baptist Church of Champaign, Illinois, responded to a request of Alcoholics Anonymous for a place to meet on Wednesday evenings. There are more alcoholics attending the AA meetings than church members at prayer meetings. Some of the Alcoholic Anonymous members have attended the church's worship services. The pastor is a member of the board of directors for a halfway house for alcoholics known as the Mustard Seed House.

Bible Classes: The Sagamore Hills Baptist Church in Ft. Worth has a Bible study class made up of people who have drinking problems. In order to make alcoholics feel comfortable in coming, the group began meeting in a garage. Five years later it moved its meeting place to the downtown mission of the church.

The class was formulated by a church member who was an alcoholic for twelve years. He had been converted in 1957 and began living for God. He gathered five other people in 1964 and began the group. The class ministered to several hundred alcoholics and problem drinkers during its first five years. Although not everyone who has attended the class has been cured of his drinking problem, results are impressive. Several class members now hold offices in the Sagamore Hill Church.

The group's philosophy is similar to Alcoholics Anonymous. The group is known as the Follow Me Bible Class, using Jesus' words.

Visitation, prayer and fellowship are ingredients in addition to the Bible study. Attention is given first to the alcoholics physical needs. This may include a trip to the hospital in the middle of the night.

The Follow Me Bible Class has proven that an alcoholic can be treated when Christians care enough to seek him.

Drug Treatment Classes

Gradual Withdrawal Approach: The Castle Hills Baptist Church of San Antonio, Texas, attempted to come to grips with the city's problem of 3,000 drug addicts.

In 1969, Dr. Ernest Gregory, a member of the church, devised a program to provide addicts with a complete reorientation to life.

A group of thirty men and women addicts met at the Castle Hills Church each week with psychologists, psychiatrists, and physicians.

The physicians place some of the addicts on the drug substitute, methadone. Before methadone, the addict had three alternatives, according to former Baptist Home Mission Board leader Warren Rawles, "He could go on as he was, try to kick the habit cold turkey, or get busted."[3]

The methadone costs only $1.50 per day, compared with $50.00 a day for a drug habit. It is estimated that 2,500 addicts in New York and 1,300 in New Orleans use methadone.

Through the efforts of the Castle Hills Baptist Church many of the men have made commitments to Christ and have begun disciplined Christian instruction. They also spend time in group therapy. Dr. Gregory gives two or three nights a week to the program.

Former pastor Jack Taylor said there is a strong motivation factor because the men can return to society with self-respect.

Immediate Withdrawal Approach: Rev. David Wilkerson located a site at 416 Clinton Avenue in Brooklyn for his Teen Challenge Center in December, 1960. Within six months the drug rehabilitation center was in full operation.

Rev. Wilkerson became alarmed that of the addicts treated at the United States Public Health Service Hospital in Lexington, sixty-four percent returned. Others estimate that eighty-five to ninety percent of all addicts return to the habit.

Teen Challenge initiated an instantaneous withdrawal. Wilkerson wrote, "We used it partly because we had no choice; we could not administer the withdrawal drugs that are used in hospitals. But we prefer cold turkey on its own merits, too. The withdrawal is considerably faster; three days as against three weeks. The pain is more intense, but it is over sooner."[4]

When an addict comes for help, he is guaranteed continual help. As one addict was told, "When we aren't with you in person, we will be with you in prayer."[5] The Center's unofficial motto is, "The Holy Spirit is in charge here."[6]

Scripture reading and prayer are a vital part of the victory over addiction. The fellowship of the Christian community offers motivation and healing.

Teen Challenge Centers are also located in Chicago, Philadelphia, Boston, Los Angeles and Toronto.

Therapy Groups

Rev. Jim Reid, Chaplain of the Las Vegas Strip, has a group therapy ministry at his office weekly. The leader has assembled a group of fifteen persons with the anticipation of four or five drop-outs.

The group began by taking the MMPI tests (Minnesota

Multiphasic Personality Inventory) and sending them in for evaluation to Cecil Osborne of Yokefellow (209 Park Avenue, Burlingame, California). The test deals with eleven areas of the individual's personality. Each member uses *Prayer Can Change Your Life*. Every two weeks each group member receives a slip in the mail from Yokefellows in reference to the MMPI test. Rev. Reid says, "The slip may say, 'you're resentful,' or 'you're hostile,' or 'you have anxiety.'"

During the group sessions, the members discuss their problems. There are six basic rules of the group including confession only of one's own sins, always speaking in the first person, speaking only of one's feelings, not theories, and nobody dominating the group.

Each member covenants that he will spend a half-hour daily in devotional reading and prayer. They pray for their own problems and for others in the group.

Alcoholics, diabetics and rheumatoid arthritis victims have been reportedly healed in the group. "Disease stems from the absence of some spiritual ingredient in one's life," Reid says.

Vocation

Churches have helped individuals secure productive employment through a diversity of classes. Some are staffed by church members, while others are located at the church house and staffed by the government. Another group approach is church initiated, but funded through government and private funding.

Church-staffed and Sponsored Classes

A Catholic Mission in Vietnam and Southern Baptist churches in Brooklyn, N.Y., and New Albany, Indiana, illustrate successful church sponsored vocational classes. Both churches have enlisted lay people to minister through their vocational skills with satisfying results.

Mechanics Class: The Graceland Baptist Church of New

Albany inaugurated a class in mechanical skills geared for teenage boys. A church member who is the owner of an engine exchange, worked with a staff member in the ministry.

The program combined vocational training with a recreational program and Bible study.

The church staff canvassed its membership to find people that would teach a variety of skills.

Key Punch Class: Park Slope Baptist Church sponsored an Adult Education Program in the summer of 1972, which enrolled 280 people in Brooklyn.

The church treasurer taught key punch operations to community women at his executive office in Manhattan. He then hired a number of the trainees. A number of families were baptized through the cultivative relationships.

Typing Classes: When Mrs. Beverly Patterson's husband was pastor and missionary at the Park Slope Baptist Church in Brooklyn she began a typing class in 1969. Many of the Spanish people in the eighty percent Catholic community were unable to qualify for good jobs.

The class was held on Saturday mornings at the church for three or four hours. The women in the class would take typing before lunch and bookkeeping afterwards. The class reached twenty members and required Mrs. Patterson to enlist other instructors from the church membership.

A typewriter company donated secondhand typewriters as a community service.

A number of Puerto Ricans taking the course were able to get improved jobs and salaries, because of this ministry. One church member who was hired for an insurance company helped class members get jobs there.

Mrs. Patterson spoke of two sisters who could only qualify as cleaning women before they enrolled. They later became filing clerks with accelerated salaries.

A number of the enrollees visited the Park Slope church. Many of these people had not even known of the church before enrolling in the program. The program was ultimately discontinued for an all-out Day Care service.

Plumbing Classes: Another member of the Park Slope Church is a plumber. Former pastor Larry Patterson arranged for him to train community adults in this vocation.

Electrical skills were incorporated in the class. The group of men in the class built offices in the church and repaired neighboring homes, as part of the training.

General Para-Professional Classes: Miss Anna Keelin directs a Baptist Center in Norfolk, Virginia. She describes her job as "being a liaison between black and white community."[7] She has initiated a group training class for para-professionals. The weekly class involves numerous unchurched ladies and builds bridges between them and the church.

Teaching Classes: The Good Shepherd Mission nuns in Vink Long, Vietnam, began a ministry in 1958 that has turned teenage thieves into teachers and typists, and bar girls into beauticians.

The nuns operated the government's only re-education center for women. In fourteen years of operation 2,000 girls received training at the convent in the heart of the Mekong Delta.

Mother Superior Bernadette Sillivan stated "We take them in, teach them a trade and when they're finished try to find jobs for them."[8]

Many women thieves and prostitutes were required to spend a year or two at the center as part of their terms.

Most of the girls attended the optional religious services at the convent. Among the variety of vocations for which people were prepared, was the teaching profession.

Church-initiated Classes With Government Staffing

Southern Baptist leaders in California made efforts to discover the greatest human needs in the westside part of Fresno and the Watts section of Los Angeles. Many people in the area were seeking better jobs. State Mission's director, Rev. Ralph Longshore, contacted the Model Cities program to arrange for an Adult Education Program to be held in two neighboring black Baptist churches.

The University of California system provided a faculty in the Baptist-owned House of Agape in Watts, Los Angeles, and Westside Baptist Church in Fresno. The University cooperation provided over $200,000 per year in faculty salaries, according to Longshore.

In one year nearly 300 underprivileged blacks and Mexicans gained employment through this ministry in Fresno. Baptists provide a modest funding of nearly $4,000 for the job training and placement.

Church-initiated Classes with Private Funding

A dynamic black pastor came to Philadelphia in the 1950's with a Christian concern that would make an impact across the nation. Rev. Leon Sullivan wanted to help his members and other black youth have fair job opportunities. The chief problem in the early 1960's was that the blacks weren't trained to obtain the available jobs as stenographers, secretaries, sheet metal workers, machinists, chemical and laboratory workers, computer operators, key punch operators, merchandisers, teletype operators and manufacturers.

Sullivan decided "if we are not prepared then we will make ourselves prepared. We will help ourselves."[9] That would be a good slogan.

On January 24, 1964, a black self-help job training program was unveiled in an abandoned north Philadelphia jailhouse known as OIC — Opportunity Industrialization Center.

Sullivan's autobiography says, "What's behind OIC? People want to know. The answer, for Leon Sullivan, is God and the contagious spirit of his church members. Their enterprises are founded on modest investments and great faith."[10]

Sullivan testifies, "The inspiration for its work came out of the Bible and the motivation for doing the things had come out of the desire...to do something to help African Americans to rise."[11]

The first courses offered were drafting, sheet metal work, machine shop, chemical laboratory technicians training, power machine operating, electronics assembly, teletype operating and restaurant practices. Over 6,000 people in Philadelphia alone passed through the OIC program and gained profitable jobs in the first six years. While federal manpower training programs require $3,600 per trainee, OIC trains a man for $1,000.

The program has scattered and was being utilized in seventy cities five years after its conception. In 1970 the Southern Baptist Convention invested $10,000 in this ministry, as a constructive effort to avert the crises in the nation.

There were 600 members of Rev. Sullivan's Zion Baptist Church who helped provide a financial base. These members pledged ten dollars a month support for OIC for 36 months in the 10-36 plan.

An orientation program was deemed necessary to help persons with low esteem adjust to a new job and life. This prevocational training was called the Feeder Program. The activity would prepare a man psychologically by building his ambition, helping his attitude, providing guidance in grooming, conduct and personal work habits.

Church Membership Classes

The Frankford Avenue Baptist Church in Philadelphia's inner city is located in an eighty percent Catholic community. When I served as pastor in 1970, I discovered many Catholic parents who were concerned because their junior and teen children had never been baptized. Catholic parents would often ask me to baptize their children. I agreed to speak to the children on the Biblical requirements for the ordinance. With the parent's consent and encouragement, nearly twenty nominally Catholic youths made personal decisions for Christ in one year.

The children who participated were already eager to be baptized. The imperative task was to provide Biblical instruction and solicit a genuine commitment to Christ. The classes dealt with the divergencies in concepts of salvation between Baptists and Catholics. The course also dealt with three and a half centuries of Baptist history. The Baptist Statement of Faith was another ingredient in the class study.

Amid the advice the nineteenth century Baptist giant Charles H. Spurgeon, gave to his students were these words,

> Hold numerous inquirer's meetings, at which the addresses shall be all intended to assist the troubled and guide the perplexed, and with these intermingle fervent prayers for the individuals present, and short testimonies from recent converts and others.[12]

This approach is still successful in creating an interest, providing information and enlisting a personal commitment to Christ.

Children's Education

Sesame Street Classes: The Frankford Avenue Baptist Church staff of Philadelphia discovered a unique opportunity for ministry in 1970. The Children's Television Workshop had a news story in the paper seeking places for Sesame Street classes to meet. The program was designed to teach preschoolers basic learning skills.

The church agreed to sponsor the activity by making its building available and providing volunteer workers. The children watch Sesame Street for the first hour, then they review the things they learned through games and activities.

Miss Brenda Forlines, former director of Church Weekday Ministries, has successfully channeled unchurched children and their parents into the church, because of this ministry.

Head Start Classes: The Valley Baptist Church of San Francisco has dramatically reached out to its community with innovative ministries.

Former Pastor Harold Parsley testified that a dying church gained new life by responding to community needs. One evidence was in opening the church building to a Head Start program.

Two Spanish Baptist churches in the city have also begun Head Start programs. The First Spanish Baptist Church has augmented a Head Start program with English classes for Spanish-speaking adults.

Day Care Classes: It is estimated that forty percent of American mothers work. This results in four million preschool children that must be placed in someone's care. There are at least a million children under age fourteen without any adult supervision, while the mothers are at work. Countless others receive only custodial care.

An increasing number of churches are responding to this need with Day Care Centers. The ministry generally refers to the care of pre-school age children between 6:00 a.m. and 6:00 p.m.

These centers are operated with the realization that a person's achievement in life largely depends on what he learned before he is four years old. Churches can offer children affection, care and guidance. They may also supply emotional, physical, social and intellectual growth.

Atlanta's Wieuca Road Baptist Church provides a day care center and kindergarten to persons who are mostly non-members. The ministry began as members realized the surplus of young marrieds and divorced parents in the community.

The Floral Park Baptist Church of Butte, Montana, has had a state-approved day-care center and kindergarten since 1970.

Mrs. Ross Harmonson, the former pastor's wife taught the kindergarten class from 9:00 to 11:30 a.m. and worked in the day-care center from 3:00 to 6:00 p.m, Monday through Friday.

There were seventeen in kindergarten and forty-two in day care in the first year.

The First Baptist Church (A.B.C.) of Merchantsville, New Jersey, recognized a need for child care provisions in their community. In 1966 they established a Nursery School and enrolled twenty-four children. They enlisted nearly twice that number the following year.

The ministry grew into a Day Care Center with urging from the State of New Jersey. Their program begins at 7:30 a.m. and extends until 5:30 p.m. The children have two periods daily of Bible stories, rest, snack time, and singing about Christ.

During the first year only forty children's families became involved in the church. Conversions and renewed Christian lives were also results of the ministry. Pastor Samuel Jeanes says, "A day care ministry provides an opportunity to find a new group of prospects for Christ."

Churches considering these ministries should follow careful procedures: (1) Elect a day-care committee; (2) The committee gathers information on license regulations; (3) Formulate staff requirements and policies (U.S. Office of Education); (4) Report committee findings to church business meeting; (5) The committee seeks help from the church in selecting a director and securing a license.

Drama

Rev. Alvin Carmines became Associate Minister of Judson Memorial Church in Greenwich Village, N.Y., in 1961. The church has a dual Baptist and Congregational heritage. He formed three diverse groups within the congregation — regular Sunday worship participants, social activists who followed the senior Baptist minister, Rev. Howard Moody, and village artists.

Carmines began an outreach to the latter group by searching for play scripts. He received forty responses the first week and the response has been as steady ever since. Many of the one act plays are produced with little cost by Judson Poet's Theater. The Theater has become "a major outlet for new theatrical talent."[13]

In the mid 1960's the congregation requested the ministers to remove the church pulpit and pews. A simple altar and folding chairs replaced the other equipment in order to provide lively Sunday services. Dance and drama are frequently included with sermons and songs during the worship experience.

Carmines estimates that nearly a third of the congregation is Jewish, with nearly another third composed of youngsters experimenting with Oriental religions.

Clubs

The diversity of clubs for involvement of residents in any community may be divided into recreational and hobby groups. While the groups may overlap in the interpersonal relations they produce, their structures will differ. These clubs have the common aim of building bridges of friendship between people and the church. The ultimate purpose is to enable children, youth and adults to experience love and concern that would encourage them to believe in and trust in Christ.

Recreation

Youth Lounge: "The Belfry" is sponsored by the St. Paul United Methodist Church in Omaha, Nebraska, weekdays from 2:30 to 5:00 p.m. at their fourth floor center. The program began when youth asked the church leaders for a place to use after school.

Associate pastor, Rev. Richard Turner, reports more non-members than members using the youth facility. Between fifteen and thirty youth visit "The Belfry" daily. Rev. Turner feels the Belfry provides a setting for youth where there is some degree of Christian community.

The pinball machine and other games are put away on weekends when church youth groups use the center.

Parents Without Partners: The international, non-sectarian, educational organization, Parents-Without-Partners, Inc., is devoted to the interests and welfare of single parents and their children. Some churches sponsor such groups at their buildings.

Southern Baptists in Louisville, Kentucky, promoted Parents Without Partners meetings in a one-minute spot announcement on the radio. There were thirty-three phone calls in one day in response to this Louisville ministry.

A church meaningfully involved with widowed or divorced adults can provide a major spiritual influence on the lives of these alienated and lonely persons.

Hobby Classes

Ceramics: A popular pastime among many housewives is ceramics. The basic elements needed are a tool grit cloth and sponge. A kiln is necessary to bake the greenware, but this can often be borrowed from elsewhere in the community.

When Baptist pastor Rev. John Tanner served in Huron, South Dakota, he located some women in his congregation who wanted a ceramics class at the church. The women brought unchurched friends to the meetings. The pastor attended the sessions himself and often brought an inspirational message.

Chess: In the summer of 1972, Bobby Fischer of the United States defeated Boris Spassky for the world's championship in chess. This brought an accelerated interest for the sport in America.

Rev. Paul Baxter, former associate pastor of the Baptist New Haven Fellowship of Christ, organized a chess class at the home of a terminally ill youth. A class of five was begun that met weekly for fellowship and inspiration. The class which was originally intended as a help for the dying youth became a ministry to every participant.

Quilting: The Calvary Baptist Church of Midland, Texas, has provided the church building for a quilting class. The women bring a sack lunch and engage in Bible study. The ministry has effectively reached a number of Latin Americans in the city.

Arts and Crafts: The Frankford Avenue Baptist Church of Philadelphia began an arts and crafts program in the summer of 1970. Mrs. Sara Potter, the pastor's wife, headed up three "Fun Time Clubs," as a follow-up to four outdoor Bible schools, which had enrolled 550 children. Some 180 Catholic children who had participated in the park activity began attending similar classes in the church building. Eventually, some 80 of the children began participating in the Sunday School as a result of this ministry. During the fall of 1970 another staff member, Miss Brenda Forlines, was added to coordinate these clubs and other activities.

While the Philadelphia congregation developed its own materials, many churches rely upon the Backyard Bible Club materials, which are available through the Baptist bookstores. The Weekday Bible Study Series also provides helps for Baptist youth from nine to sixteen years of age, and are available throughout Baptist bookstores.

Southern Baptists in Chelsea, Massachusetts, have instituted "Happy Time" clubs for children from five to twelve years of age. Bible stories, music, games, crafts, and refreshments are the basic elements.

A "Charlie Brown-Snoopy Club" has been launched by the Brookhaven Baptist Church of Decatur, Georgia. This church with 85 enrolled in Sunday School has responded to the nationwide popularity of Charlie Brown and named a children's club after him.

The club is designed for boys and girls in grades one through six. The children meet every Friday after school from 3:30 to 5:00 p.m. The youth are encouraged to bring their unchurched friends to the meeting.

Pastor Wayne Fields reports that music, Bible Study, recreation and refreshments are combined in the ministry.

The club has one special event each month such as a trip to the zoo or a wiener roast. The children also put on a "County fair" where they used play money they had earned to buy games, food and drink.

Photography: Sam Satterfield, minister to Youth at First Baptist Church of Corpus Christi, Texas, began a photography club. He proposed that members of the church be invited to bring friends for instruction in the class. Efforts have been to cultivate the friendship of unchurched individuals for eventual commitment to Christ.

Dominoes: Senior Citizens in Nebraska City, Nebraska, have responded to a church offering the popular domino activity. Each Tuesday evening many elderly adults meet for domino games at the Faith Baptist Church. None of the participants are members of the church, and all are prospects. Bridges of friendship were built between these adults and the church, according to former Pastor Michael McDowell.

Skydiving: A suburban Omaha skydiving director contacted a Baptist pastor about meeting classes in his church. The former pastor, Rev. R.C. Rayner, of the Harrison Street Baptist Church was delighted to make his building available to the group.

The class met at the church once a week for classroom instructions, prior to actual skydiving experiences. Many of those attending the class were unchurched. The pastor cultivated the friendship of those attending the class, and several people began attending church services through this contact.

Ham Radio: A deacon at the Bethel Baptist Church in Scottsbluff wanted to begin a class for ham operators. Pastor William Tritten agreed to support the ministry.

One night a week the deacon invited potential ham operators to the church for class instruction. Many in the group were unchurched people. Following the teaching period refreshments were served and group members were invited to remain for Bible study.

Athletic

Weight-Lifting: The Metropolitan Baptist Church of Cambridge, Massachusetts, has a widespread set of youth ministries.

Several years ago the church initiated weight-lifting instruction for teenage boys. The pastor of the multiple staff is Dr. John Houghston. He diligently encourages the use of diverse and creative methods of befriending unchurched people.

Bowling: Church bowling leagues have gained increased popularity in recent years. The First Baptist Church of Bellevue, Nebraska, has a team entered in a community league. Though the teams are generally composed of church members, the First Church of Bellevue has reached unchurched people through this ministry. These non-members are officers of the church's team, and a number of them have begun attending the church because of this association.

Basketball: Church basketball and baseball league teams have long been an effective means of reaching unchurched youth. Children on the team become conscientious about enlisting friends with athletic ability. Unchurched youth often respond to the opportunity, even if occasional church attendance is a requirement for playing.

Rev. Harold Manahan organized three basketball teams at the Chandler Acres Baptist Church in Omaha. One is an open team of men and high schoolers. The other two teams work out on Saturdays at a community gym. This team play has served successfully as a vehicle of church outreach.

INNOVATIVE INDOOR MINISTRIES

Christian witnessing may transpire wherever people assemble. Churches may provide ministries with this concept in mind. The diversity of locations and human need will dictate the most effective ministry to be utilized. This chapter presents proven types of cultivative ministries for more than twenty indoor settings. Those creative efforts should provide stimulation to thoughtful church leaders. Some leaders may feel the challenge for duplicating some of these ministries in similar indoor locations in their cities. Others will react from these illustrations with an insight for initiating a project in unique indoor situations in their own communities.

Conversing

Bible Study Fellowships: Unchurched adults across the nation are meeting with increasing frequency in informal church-sponsored Bible studies. The groups go by many names, and the format is varied. The common denominator of these gatherings is that a caring fellowship of persons are searching for God in Bible study and dialogue.

The chief impact of a Bible Fellowship is in the spontaneous free-wheeling discussions. Everyday personal problems which bear down on the participants can be ventilated as the Scripture lesson relates to their lives.

A free atmosphere in which people agree to disagree is the key to vital interchange of feelings and views. The use of a modern translation of the Bible, such as *Good News For Modern Man*, helps novices comprehend the Scripture. When I've led groups, I remind Catholic participants of a quote from Father Louis F. Hartman, C.SS.R. executive director of the Catholic Biblical Association. He told the traditionally

Protestant Advisory Council of the American Bible Society, "I would be happy to see the Today's English version in the home of every Catholic — and have him read it."[1]

One format of a Bible Study Fellowship suggested by the Home Mission Board includes,

"— For about 3 minutes have prayer (silent or spoken)
— For about 10 minutes read a Bible passage and possibly say by whom, to whom, and why it was written.
— For about 15 minutes discuss what each person present says the passage means to him.
— For about 15 minutes discuss what each person thinks he should do about it.
— For about 15 minutes discuss the actions by which each person can do what he has said he should.
— For about 2 minutes have dismissal prayer (silent or spoken."

The variations to these suggestions are unlimited. The primary guideline is to avoid a lecture or monopoly by a few persons, that would hamper maximum participation by all.

The Free Methodist publication, *The Light and Life*, has suggested ways to motivate members to open their homes for Bible Study Fellowships. "Begin by making a positive commitment to God of an hour or two in your home each week. And then overcome the fear of refusal and 'what people will think' by marshaling your neighbors to your home for coffee, sharing and Bible study."[2]

The Baptist Home Mission Board has prepared materials on launching a Bible Fellowship Study Campaign that could saturate a community with the Gospel. The Church Extension Department can supply materials (1350 Spring St., N.W., Atlanta, Ga., 30309). Materials have been compiled on ways to prepare a church, the community, implement the studies, and have a proper follow-up.

Innumerable indoor settings have been the scene of an informal discussion of the Bible. Some of these locations include:

Military Base

Laymen at the First Baptist Church of Bellevue, Nebraska, conduct a weekly Bible Fellowship at the Strategic Air Command Base. Once each week at noon, these laymen and their interested friends have an informal Bible study at the nerve-center of the nation's military defense system. This witness of concerned military laymen has influenced the conversion and baptism of many Air Force personnel.

Similarly, at the National Aeronautics Space Administration (NASA) at least six Bible Fellowships are led by lay leaders of a local church. Laymen of the Park Avenue Baptist Church of Titusville, Florida, have led men to Christ in the NASA facility. One electrical engineer, Eldon Raley, who is working on the Saturn booster project, Skylab, began meeting with a troubled friend for prayer at lunch. The group enlarged when others heard of the meeting, until 15 were involved.

Offshore Oil Rig

Kirby Doughdrill of Prentiss, Mississippi, is one of thousands of men who work on offshore drilling rigs around the world. His crew is on the drill barge seven consecutive days. He once overheard some of the members of his crew discussing the morality of capital punishment. He suggested that the men look to the Bible for insight and answers.

The Baptist layman then suggested that they begin a regular Bible study. He followed his Sunday School lessons as a guide. The group averages eight persons each Sunday when they are aboard the barge.

College Classroom

I served as Protestant Chaplain of the Temple University football team in Philadelphia from 1968-71. During this time a group of the players began attending an evening Bible Fellowship I was leading in a classroom at neighboring Messiah College. A half dozen athletes and three or four girls met weekly for several months for Bible study and discussion. Several in the group developed a more vital relationship with the church through the group fellowship.

Night Club

Jim Reid, Chaplain of the Strip in Los Angeles conducts Bible study groups backstage in night clubs. Through personal friendships he's developed with performers in the famed shows, many have been led to Christ through Bible study groups. A group of half a dozen persons sit backstage between shows with copies of *Good News For Modern Man* and search for Biblical truth.

Ranch House

Several years ago Rev. and Mrs. Dewey Hickey of First Baptist Church in Valentine, Nebraska, found a ranch owner with many helpers who were interested in Bible study in the Sandhills. They traveled nearly 200 miles round-trip every Friday night to meet with about 25 people in the ranch house. The pastor's wife took the children into the bedroom and presented them a Sunday School lesson. Rev. Hickey informally conversed with the ranch hands and led many to Christ.

Business Building

A group of Baptist laymen meet once a week at lunch for Bible study in an office building in downtown Manhattan, N.Y. They assemble in the office of the Metropolitan Baptist Association, which is convenient to their vocational offices. These laymen have a potential of bringing unchurched business colleagues to an experience with Christ through this Bible study.

Apartments

A Baptist couple who lived in an apartment outside

Philadelphia agreed to open up their apartment one night a week for Bible study. The couple neither knew their neighbors, nor knew how to recruit participants. Leaflets were distributed beneath the front doors of this multi-unit apartment complex. Some half dozen couples soon responded and participated in the Bible Fellowship group. Strangers became acquainted and vital friendships developed. Some of the couples soon began attending church with the Baptist family.

City Homes

A group of college students from Indiana University spent a mid-semester break in Philadelphia during the winter of 1968. They visited over 1,000 homes in the non-evangelical northeast section of the city. They asked the residents if they might have any interest in an informal Bible study among neighbors one night a week. Surprisingly, over 100 persons expressed a tentative interest. Three groups were formed in scattered locations. There were ultimately about 30 couples who followed through and participated. Two of the groups were unsuccessful. The third group of eight to twelve persons met for a year and a half and eventually became the nucleus for a church.

Church Basement

The Park Slope Baptist Church of Brooklyn had a basement which was regularly utilized for a ministry to unchurched youths. One night each weekend it was a coffeehouse and another night it was used for dances. Pastor Larry Patterson would encourage the youth to enjoy the unstructured activities from 8 to 11 p.m. Then the youth were informed that the pastor was going to lead a Bible study. Any youth interested in the study were invited to remain another hour while the others left. Generally, 50 of the 200 youth present would remain to hear the pastor 'rap" from *Good News For Modern Man*.

Coffeehouses

Beach House: "The Anchor" is a Christian coffeehouse on the Gulf of Mexico, sponsored by the neighboring First Baptist Church of Lake Jackson, Texas. Over six thousand teens visit the coffeehouse each summer. There are generally 100 persons present each night its in operation. The sponsoring church provides the finances and manpower that is necessary to operate this beach ministry.

The emphasis is strong on personal evangelism. There are a large number of runaway youth who have been helped through this ministry. Other lonely, drug addicted and depressed youth have also received assistance at the beach coffeehouse.

Village House: "The Infinite Dimension" is a coffeehouse operated by Central Baptist Church of Virginia's Piedmont Association in Lowesville, a town of 456 people. Church youth sought and received permission to renovate an old frame house on church property.

The three reasons for undertaking the ministry were: (1) to reach unchurched youth; (2) to encourage the participation of existing church youth; (3) to provide a place of fellowship. The coffeehouse ministry is credited with a positive influence on the lives of many youth, since it began in December, 1970.

City House: "His Place" is a coffeehouse located in a white frame house in Bellevue, Nebraska. The young military personnel at the Strategic Air Command Base find it a place for relaxing fellowship. Pastor of the First Baptist Church, Rev. Charles Hawley, and Associate Minister, Glyn St. Andre, mingle informally with the young servicemen. The pastor has found a good rapport there with people who never would have attended a Baptist church otherwise. He has had a number of men accept Christ and later baptized through the contacts of the coffeehouse.

Storefront Building: Rev. Duane McCormick operated the Baptist-sponsored "One-Way Place" in Omaha's inner city for several years. A storefront building was rented in the black community with impressive results.

Nearly a hundred youth would come for the fellowship with other teens. The unstructed atmosphere gave opportunity for Christian workers to initiate friendship with the participants. The ministry closed after several years of operation due to the excessive demands on the pastor's time.

Church Basement: The "Lost and Found" meets in the basement of Worcester Baptist Church in Worcester, Massachusetts. Former pastor, Rev. Bob Tremaine had a group of concerned adults to mingle at the table with youth during rock and folk music group presentations. Between musical portions of the program, Rev. Tremaine led in a rap session on the Biblical teaching on contemporary issues.

Many youth have been led to Christ through the informal private dialogues at the tables. New church members would serve the tables. On some nights as many as 150 people waited outside to come in.

The Frankford Avenue Baptist Church began the "Icthus," a coffeehouse ministry in its basement in the summer of 1971. Teenage gang members were befriended, and helped renovate the basement. Community youth who played in band groups were invited to perform. Attendance soared to 100 people nightly when the rock groups played.

Through interpersonal relationships several dozen teens were won to Christ in the coffeehouse the first year. After the Icthus had been in operation for over five months, guests were invited in to lead serious conversations with the group. In December, 1970, a group of four from Philadelphia Teen Challenge came to speak. Two of the visitors were reformed drug addicts who were cured after a conversion to Christ. The usually sarcastic and troublesome crowd became strangely gripped by these testimonies. About a dozen persons accepted Christ later that night in small group settings.

Studying

Reading Room Concept: The Christian Scientist denomination has blossomed across the nation largely because of reading rooms. On the main streets of the largest cities and in the most elite shopping malls, a Christian Science Reading Room can be found. The availability of selective literature, the provision of a studious atmosphere, and the counsel of trained leaders has produced results.

People drop in the business office that would never attend church. Evangelical Christian churches have a great deal to learn from this market place ministry.

Library Ministry: Rev. Gordon Thomas initiated an innovative ministry in the Northwood Park Shopping Center in Lewiston, Maine. His headquarters, "The Chapel," meets in a 12 by 60 foot mobile chapel. It is divided into an office, a prayer chapel and a library. The Church Library Department of the Sunday School Board provided the library as an experimental project.

The library contains some novels and ministries. The pastor ordered books to offer understanding and comfort to people who are troubled with spiritual and emotional problems.

Rev. Thomas frequently discovers the hobby of merchants and visitors. He frequently provides them a book from the library. This effort cultivated deeper friendship by showing the ministers care for the total person. Rev. Thomas maintains "The 'Cross in the Marketplace' is not a new idea." The cross of the Chapel...was erected because people crowd the marketplaces and the cross needs to be where the people are."

Book Store Ministry: Rev. Harry Bristow operates the non-denominational Christian Cinema Bookstore of Jenkintown, Pennsylvania. The friendly and informal atmosphere of the bookstore lends itself to Christian witnessing. Rev. Bristow mingles with the customers and has had frequent opportunities to lead customers to Christ. The customers' natural questions concerning content of books open the doors for deeper sharing.

Book Review: The Park Cities Baptist Church of Dallas has a fellowship gathering with a book review period. It is a get-acquainted coffee for cultivating visitors of all ages to the church. In 1970 the initial coffee and book review drew more than 300 persons, 50 of whom were guests.

During the first 45 minutes the group visit and enjoy refreshments. The guests were welcomed by the pastor. A book review of a religious novel followed.

Sunday School: During the greatest period of Southern Baptist church expansion, ninety percent of the people that were baptized came through the Sunday School.

However, Sunday School enrollment declined nine percent in 1970 from 41 million to just over 37 million for all Protestants. Southern Baptists had withstood the declining trend, but they suffered enrollment setbacks for four years in a row.

Sunday School Secretary Arthur Flake developed some laws of growth that have bolstered Baptists for over half a century. Flake insisted that the churches must locate the unchurched prospects that are available. The church then must provide adequate facilities for the total number of possibilities. The next responsibility is to enroll the prospects in groupings that do not exceed certain proven limits. The Sunday School should seek to involve all participants in the activities of the church, through cultivative visitation. The church then seeks to activate the participant with his own ministry of service for Christ.

The ACTION plan for Sunday School enrollment outreach ministry was devised by Rev. E.S. Andy Anderson of the Riverside Baptist Church in Ft. Myers, Florida. In 1975 the Baptist Sunday School Department of Nashville adopted the outreach plan for the churches of the denomination.

Anderson discovered in Ft. Myers that only forty percent of the Sunday School members were present on any given Sunday. He learned that this statistic was true across the nation.

His conclusion was that since the percentage of attendance remained constant, growth came with increased enrollment. For every additional hundred persons enrolled, he discovered that about forty would become active participants in the Sunday School.

The ACTION plan involves an intensive one week enrollment campaign at several intervals during the year. During these enrollment campaigns, Sunday School workers go out in the streets to recruit candidates for Bible study. The workers go door-to-door and into shopping malls. The pastor also makes a concerted effort to enroll members for Bible Study who are not in the Sunday School program.

The ACTION materials include three manuals and a ninety minute cassette recording. They are available through the General Officer's Section of the Sunday School Board in Nashville.

Anderson has utilized the same concept to begin new missions. A host of Christian workers are into the streets in a community in which they wish to begin a new mission. When two hundred individuals have been enrolled for the new Sunday School, the leaders can be confident that eighty will participate.

Former Baptist Sunday School leader, J.N. Barnette made many key observations for effective Bible study. He suggested that enrollment increases when there is a worker for every eight class members. He discovered that new units grow faster and win more, but reach their peak a few months after their beginning. He also learned that enrollment and attendance increase on the basis of actual cultivative visits made. Barnette also said, "The building sets the pattern."[3]

The basic concept is: begin with the need, move to leadership, then to space. The cycle then repeats itself.

Vacation Bible School

Local Church Building: The name, Vacation Bible School, may not attract non-evangelicals to come to a Baptist Church for the initial visit. However, when children have had a previous pleasant contact with the church, a VBS may evoke a positive response. A Vacation Bible School provides an intensive week of cultivation for unchurched children.

A VBS may serve as a first contact with children from a Protestant background. It may also serve as a means of "follow-up cultivation" for persons of either Protestant or Catholic persuasion.

It is quite helpful if the actual church Sunday School teachers meet the children in a similar VBS age group. This enhances the transition process for the unchurched youth to the church fellowship.

Counseling

In Shopping Centers: In Winston-Salem, N. C., the associate pastor of the Knollwood Baptist Church spends fifteen hours a week counseling in a shopping center.

Rev. George Colgin emphasized that the merchants association asked him to consider serving as chaplain. The minister had cards printed listing him simply as "counselor", and left them at cash registers around the shopping center. He had regular coffee breaks at a steakhouse and kept office hours in a real estate office.

When Rev. Gordon Thomas began his shopping center ministry in Lewistown, Maine, his main emphasis was counseling. He attempted to maintain hours from 9 a.m. to 9 p.m. Initially many people came out of curiosity. Later, he used other means of making himself known and available to the people when the curiosity waned.

Race Track: Mike Eyer served as a US-2 (two years in service in the United States) in Philadelphia for the Baptist Home Mission Board. At the end of his tenure several Protestant denominations were concerned with providing a ministry to the area race track personnel. A non-profit corporation was formed and Mr. Eyer was named Christian chaplain to minister to the six to eight hundred people who live, work, eat and sleep in the area.

Mike walked around the stable every day to speak to everyone and establish relationships of trust. These visits provided numerous opportunities for counseling.

He served at Atlantic City's Garden State Race Track in September and October. During December and January he ministered at Philadelphia's Liberty Bell Track.

Apartment House: The 1970 census showed 18,835,646 multi-unit housing structures in America which are mainly apartments. This was an increase of 36.5 percent during the decade. New ideas for penetrating these apartments are in demand. Philadelphia's Methodist minister, Bobby G. Boyd, was partly supported by his denomination's Eastern Pennsylvania Conference. Doormen and telephone operators have begun to trust "apartment ministers." These employees inform him of the illness and grief occupants are experiencing.

Rev. Boyd found many residents who seem to have no problems. After casual conversation some begin sharing needs for employment and friends, while others are suffering from a divorce or loved one's death. Boyd said, "Maybe I can help someone get a job, or get medical attention. But mainly, I just listen, that's my Christian mission."[4]

Jails: Baptist minister, Duane McCormick, is also chaplain of the Douglas County jails. He has enlisted a number of laymen from Omaha's Chandler Acres Baptist Church to counsel with troubled prisoners. He has discovered that the inmates are highly receptive to discussing personal spiritual concerns in jail. Through the counseling efforts of these men, over 100 men accepted Christ in a single year.

YMCA: Southern Baptists have provided weekly worship services at the downtown Philadelphia YMCA since 1968. A group of less than a dozen persons are normally in attendance. One Sunday evening I preached to only nine people. It seemed like an uneventful experience. However, at the close of the service, three people needed counseling immediately. One was a disruptive individual who had been drinking heavily. Another was troubled by a secret drinking problem. The third was a youth who would soon need to amputate his hand.

The counseling opportunities at a YMCA are unlimited. The usual residents are mature working women and transient youths.

Night Clubs: In Louisville, Kentucky, former seminary student, Russell Waldrop, used to dress in a clerical collar and go from bar to bar at night. He offered the night people a "listening ear," as well as Christian counsel. Sometimes he discovered other needs for which he could supply or refer help. In the larger cities, there are many in this subculture of night people who sleep during the day and can only work and be helped at night.

Hotel: Dr. John W. Hughston is a volunteer chaplain in the Holiday Inns, Inc. Chaplain on Call program. He serves as pastor of the Metropolitan Baptist Church in Cambridge, Mass.

Throughout the nation, cards printed with the Chaplain-on-Call number are left in Holiday Inn rooms. A minister is always available to answer a call from anyone in need.

The non-denominational program was begun through the motel chain headquarter's Office of Chaplain in 1969.

Dr. Hughston received the first Chaplain-on-Call merit award from Holiday Inn. He says, "The principal value of the Chaplain-on-Call program lies in the fact that the printed card in the hotel or motel suggests to a troubled traveler that this kind of contact would be helpful."[5]

Feeding

There are an estimated 450 rescue missions across North America. In 1971 there were twelve new rescue missions joining the umbrella organizations, the International Union of Gospel Mission.

The organization's president, Jerry Dunn, says that a fourth of the persons they help recover. The rescue missions served 14 million meals in North America during 1971.

Nearly all missions require persons who are fed to attend worship services. The mission directors insist that the spiritual help is far more important than food or shelters. They say, "If we don't give them a foundation to build their lives on, we give them nothing."

General Manager, Arthur Bestnater of Los Angeles Union Rescue Mission reports a startling drop in the average age of derelicts. In the early 1960's the average derelict was in his upper 50's. Today, due to the drug culture Bestnater says they are in their lower 30's.

The Baptist Rescue Mission in New Orleans ministers to 6,000 men a month. Most of these persons are in their forties and have an alcohol problem. The mission gives a man a hot meal, clothing and a place to sleep. If he responds to the alcohol clinic, the mission helps him get a job. Assistant Director, Eugene Rrieger, says, "Our goal is for each man to realize the potential of Christ in his life."

Performing

Church Building

Style Show: The Park Avenue Baptist Church of Titusville, Florida, has held a style show as a means of Christian witnessing. The church women's group sold 200 tickets to a style show at a dinner in the church gym. They arranged the fashion presentation with a local department store. A Christian leader gave her testimony for Christ to the audience which included many unchurched people at the conclusion.

Restaurant

Musical Presentation: Pete Nunez, a former Baptist pastor and evangelistic singer, has become a part of the program for Radford's Cafeteria in Dallas. Nunez sings pop numbers and songs with a Christian message on Sunday afternoons.

Lounge

Musical Presentation: Rev. Frank Scott, pastor of the Gateway Baptist Church in Pittsburgh, has formed a singing duo with another church member. They are called "The Phoenix." A popular downtown Pittsburgh lounge, the Grogshop, invited the duo to perform for two weeks in 1972. The men sang six nights a week for four or five hours. Then they spent their hourly breaks sharing Christ with the customers at the tables.

Christian entertainer, Pat Boone, his wife and four daughters surprised many people by performing at a Playboy Club during 1972. Boone's response was that they would appear any place they could sing their spiritual selections and bear a Christian testimony.

Night Club

Evangelistic Bob Harrington befriended and led a San Antonio night club owner to Christ several years ago. The owner changed his club into a Christian night club, The Green Gate Club. While the club was once known for strip shows, it now features Christian singers. Young performers who have performed at larger Las Vegas clubs bear a testimony for Christ to a unique audience.

Playing

Shopping Center: The Acedemy Gardens Baptist Chapel/Center was begun in a shopping center building in November, 1968. The storefront was located in a middle income community near an elementary school. Children's arts and crafts clubs were set to coincide with the close of school three afternoons a week.

Rev. Dan Grubb and I opened the building each Wednesday night for teenage recreation. We purchased a hockey game, a ping pong table, checker boards and other focal points for entertainment. We began showing films in an effort to initiate a deeper level of spiritual dialogue. The attendance varied from twenty to thirty each week. Through this ministry, friendships developed and opportunities for counseling occurred.

While Rev. Ken Lyle was serving as pastor of the Central Nassau Baptist Church on Long Island, N.Y., the church rented a shopping center building. It was called "The Arena" and was located near a high school. The facilities included a pool table and other recreational equipment. Rev. Lyle reported that the youth learned to trust the church leaders over a period of months. The establishment of trust necessarily precedes effective Christian witnessing.

Church Property: Miss Brenda Forlines, former director of Weekday Ministries at Philadelphia's Frankford Avenue Baptist Church began a Thursday night recreation program in a church assembly room. The ministry came in response of younger teens to the church coffeehouse. The diversity of maturity from the childish younger teens to the sophisticated older teens required a solution. The youth below fifteen years were excluded from the coffeehouse, but given a Thursday night recreation opportunity.

The unstructured activity included ping pong, shuffleboard and table games. This ministry proved successful in befriending the younger teens and also keeping the older teens happy.

Center: Weekday ministries in Denver, Colorado, were formerly led by Miss Mildred Streeter. On Saturday afternoons she directed a program consisting of crafts, singing and recreation. The recreation varied from wrestling, tumbling, basketball, volleyball, table tennis, shuffleboard and various table games. The youth range from four to nineteen years, but most of them were above eight.

Rev. Larry Gardner reports about 50 volunteer helpers for the 200 people his Cincinnati center reaches each week.

There are Baptist centers in at least 23 states and the District of Columbia to meet human need. They generally combine recreation, crafts, and personal services with a study of the Bible.

Worshiping

Church Building

Dr. Lewis Rhodes, pastor of the Broadway Baptist Church in Knoxville, Tennessee, published an article in his church newsletter in 1972 on the kind of church he desired for his family. He described the importance of a sensitive minister, a caring congregation, as well as a prayerful and ministering church.

The quality of worship was also mentioned as a deciding factor, "I would look for a church with quality worship. Reverence is essential to worship. I would want a minister with dignity without pomp. I would look for good music, music that moves more than the body and words true to the Holy Scripture and our common life. I would look for a worship with a minimum of commercials."

Rev. John Bisagno, pastor of the First Baptist Church of Houston, baptized more people than any Southern Baptist in history during 1971. Bisagno has offered several suggestions for capitalizing on Sunday morning services:

"Plan for evangelism on Sunday morning. Preach it, sing it,

talk it, think it, expect it. . . .

Create a warm, relaxed atmosphere in which the lost will not feel he is doing something out of place in the pomp and pagentry of it all by walking down the aisle. . .

The music must be warm and appealing. Stuffy music will kill a church and cost you souls every Sunday.

Make the preaching simple, understandable, and finish with evangelism. . .

Begin the invitation with an appeal to the lost. . .

Extend the invitation and don't apologize for doing so. . .

Make much of those who come. . ."[6]

Nearly a thousand of Bisagno's baptisms were as a result of the Spireno crusade in Houston. In June, 1971, the church reported an average of two families a Sunday joining because their children were saved in the crusade. The church was averaging only 500 on Sunday mornings when he began pastoring early in 1970. By mid-1970 there were over 2,000 in preaching services.

An effective sermon needn't be a loud one. Outside the "Bible Belt" unchurched people are not impressed by loudness, but with sincerity.

Theaters

For over 55 years the First Baptist Church of Dallas has conducted preaching services in a movie theater during pre-Easter week.

These services were initiated by George W. Truett at the 2400 seat Palace Theater in downtown Dallas in 1919. The services are held in the theater at noon, Monday through Friday. The sermons are always brief, because of the abbreviated lunch hour.

Dr. W.A. Criswell, the current pastor, has led the worship services at the Palace since 1944. His books, *Five Great Questions of the Bible* and *Five Great Affirmations of the Bible* are based on his sermons there.

Night Clubs

When Bob Harrington is in New Orleans on Sundays, he preaches at the Sho-Bar nightclub. This establishment is across the street from his headquarters. The Sho-Bar features strippers as the normal attraction, and is run by the brother of Carlos Marcello, head of the Louisiana Mafia. On occasions a woman who was a stripper, remains clothed and sings "What A Friend We Have In Jesus." The owner said, "He's trying to save people, help people."

Shopping Centers

"The Chapel" in a Lewistown, Maine shopping center is used on Sundays for worship. The congregation is made up exclusively of native New Englanders. Between 1968 and 1970 there were as many as 75 persons attending each week. The congregation worships in a mobile chapel. Those who worship in the shopping center include persons Rev. Gordon Thomas has counseled, loaned books to, or visited in neighboring states during the week.

Race Tracks

Horse Race Ministry: Mike Eyer, minister to the Garden State and Liberty Bell Race Tracks, schedules worship sevices for the six to eight hundred people who live in the stable area. He has invited outside churches in to the stable area to conduct services. One Christian motorcycle group led services. On another occasion members of a Hebrew Christian commune were in charge of worship. The chapel services began in the spacious secretary's office on Thursdays. Initially, only a handful were attending, but the group has grown to thirty-five persons.

Race Car Ministry: Race drivers from Darlington, S.C., to College Station attend services at a mobile chapel early Sunday mornings. Bill Frazier, a Darlington evangelist, began the ministry in 1969 with a congregation of seven people. The drivers and the crews are Frazier's main concerns.

His half-hour worship service is conducted from a small chapel on the trailer Frazier uses. He attended thirty NASCAR races in 1970.

Recently, he acquired a public address system which enables everyone at the track to hear his services.

School Auditorium

High School: A church-centered evangelistic team called **SPIRENO** (Spiritual Revolution Now) was formerly led by Richard Hogue. The team has a professional sounding, easy rock trio that performs at high schools. Rev. John Bisagno explains the response, "These kids are hungry for the gospel. All that has offered them peace and love — education, sex, materialism, drugs — has failed."

Hogue billed himself as the Electric Evangelist. His group, called "Dove" performed in eighty percent of Houston's junior high schools with the rock-rhythm "Jesus Music." There were 11,000 decisions (4,000 conversions) in a four month period in Houston.

The "Phoenix" singing duo of the Gateway Baptist Church in Pittsburgh sang in a week of high school assemblies in 1971. They performed for 7,000 students in 12 assemblies. Each show closed with a witness for Christ as the alternative to drug use.

College: A phenomenal event began at Ashbury College on February 3, 1970. An eight day non-stop revival began at Hughes Auditorium in Wilmore, Kentucky. The revival lasted for 185 consecutive hours.

The unique revival spread to over 130 colleges and seminaries throughout Canada and the United States. Many of those in attendance shared personal testimonies of changed lives, that had occurred during the week.

Dramatic revivals had occurred before at Ashbury in 1950 and 1958. However, on neither occasion did the meetings extend so long without some break.

CREATIVE OUTDOOR MINISTRIES

Christian churches have seen remarkable results when they moved beyond the doors of their churches and into the community. Neutral outdoor sites have provided the setting for meaningful confrontations of the Gospel. Generally speaking, outdoor ministries can be divided into recreation and worship approaches.

Recreational Programs

Neighborhood Recreation Program: During the summer of 1968 two summer missionaries were appointed to assist me in initiating new mission work in Philadelphia. The original plan was to hold Vacation Bible Schools across the city and discover a core of interested persons.

The first target area was located in an eighty percent Catholic community of Northeast Philadelphia with only a sparse evangelical witness. The summer missionaries visited over 1200 homes to inform neighbors of a Bible School the following week. On the designated day no one came.

Disparingly, we searched for an alternative approach. Someone remembered that years before in Absecan, New Jersey, Baptists had good success by changing the name of the activity. That same day the summer missionaries returned to the streets of another community that was also heavily non-evangelical. After a week's infiltration in that community with word of an impending "Neighborhood Recreation Program." success was imminent.

The following Monday morning 130 children merged upon the designated backyard. What was the difference in the results of the two Mondays?

During the second week leaflets were passed out, stating, "Neighborhood Recreation Program — Ages Four Through Twelve — Recreation, Refreshments, Arts and Crafts, Bible Study — From 9 a.m. til 12 noon at 3407 Filter Street." In the actual activity time the children received at least thirty minutes of Bible Study. One hundred and fifty children were involved within five days. At the end of the week many of the Catholic children wanted us to come back the following week.

However, we were scheduled to repeat the process in another neighboring community the following week. Over eighty children participated during the second week. Therefore, we had achieved close-knit relationships with over 230 children from at least 150 families in two weeks. Many of the children's parents would be cultivated through the months to come into our Bible Fellowships and church services.

In 1970 in the Kensington area of Philadelphia the Home Mission Board invested in a building that another denomination had deserted. There was a church building, but few in the congregation! The church was called Frankford Avenue Baptist Chapel. That summer we planned four Neighborhood Recreation Programs in parks within a half mile of the church in all directions. The community is about seventy percent Catholic. After four successive weeks of N.R.P.'s (affectionately called "nerps" by our summer missionaries), our little chapel with twenty-nine members had enrolled 550 in Outdoor Bible school.

In the summer of 1971 the same Baptist Chapel enrolled 560 in only three Neighborhood Recreation Programs.

Subsequent visits by the church staff to the homes of these children resulted in a "royal welcome." The Catholic parents were delighted to meet the ministers who'd provided their children with a meaningful experience. The follow-up visits involved furnishing details of arts and crafts activities for the children at our church. We would inform the parents that we also had an activity in which they might wish to participate. We would inform them of an existing or projected Bible Fellowship study.

Bible School at Catholic Site: Missionary Ken Prickett who formerly served at the Indian Hall Baptist Center in Santa Fe, New Mexico, held a Bible school at a Catholic monastery in 1971. Student helpers went to the Benedictine Monastery at Pecos to initiate a cooperative ministry for community children. There were 36 children who attended in the outdoor program on monastery property.

The results were so productive that a twice weekly day camp continued throughout the summer. A priest commented, "We were awakened to the idea that the Holy Spirit should be active in our lives."[1]

Ongoing Park Program: "The "Play for Prospects" outreach plan was a ministry proposed in Sunday School Board material to reach unchurched children. Church leaders would reach out and discover parks and playground areas where children could be located and befriended. The members would contact persons in their area and express interest in enrolling the children in Sunday School or Vacation Bible School. The recreational directors, parents or baby sitters could contact persons to assist the members.

Posters placed in park areas with the director's permission help to enroll neighborhood children in these church activities. Handbills with invitations and information can also be distributed to the children.

Athletic Clinics: Southern Baptists in the Minneapolis-St. Paul area conducted Christian Baseball Clinics in thirty-three parks and twelve churches during the summer of 1970. Ex-Minnesota Twins pitcher Al Worthington conducted the baseball clinics with assistance from summer workers and pastors.

After Worthington had spent an hour explaining fundamentals of baseball to the youth and some parents, he spoke of his experience with Christ. Over 10,000 youth were enrolled in the Minnesota-Wisconsin region. As many as three or four clinics were held daily at different locations, according to Northland Baptist associational missionary, Warren Littleford.

Race Track Visitation: Mike Eyer served as Southern Baptist race track chaplain for Philadelphia and Atlantic City. His ministry included visitation of the 600-800 spiritually neglected exercise boys at the stable area. These daily visits provide an opportunity for Christian counseling. He enlists many persons he visits in weekly worship and Bible study.

Eyer's counseling has helped him learn the needs of the stable workers. They are concerned over poor living conditions, and the absence of recreational and laundry facilities.

Camp Grounds Witnessing: Baptist pastor, James Steele, initiated a cooperative inter-denominational ministry at New Jersey's largest park in 1968. He coordinated efforts of several churches to minister at the Bass River State Park. Rev. Joel Land followed Steele as pastor of the Mystic Islands Baptist Church in 1969 and continued the ministry. Land later became a staff member of the Baptist Home Mission Board and helped develop "Campers on Mission." Over 5,000 families have joined this camper's witnessing fellowship.

Campfire Sing-a-Long

A key witnessing activity at Bass River Park and elsewhere is the campfire sing-a-long. An impromptu singing session is generally led by a youth with a guitar.

Popular songs are used including ' Amen" from "Lilies of the Field."

Motion Picture Presentation

Land has also utilized motion pictures at camp. They have

good popularity because campers seldom have television and are suffering "TV-withdrawal pangs."

Moody Bible Institute's "Sermons from Science" are often used. These may be rented for $20 from a Christian Book Store.

Beach Sharing: Baptist students formed a Christian sharing group known as "God Squad" in 1970. The youth worked at Jekyll Island, a beach resort off the Georgia coast.

Rapping Sessions

The three Christian students "rapped" with the young people about their problems. One worker explained "Having somebody to 'rap with' is most important when the only other recourse is to write a letter home...which is a one-way sort of thing." They set up a tent on the beach as a coffee-house setting.

Making Friends Informally

Fifty youth, including a group known as the MIL (Meaning In Life) Singers, ministered on Daytona beaches during Easter 1968. They spent all day on the beaches making friends of visiting students. They mingled with the youth, sharing their victories and problems.

Day Camp

The First Baptist Church of Brunswick, Georgia, provides a beach ministry at Jekyll Island. They held a Day Camp each day of the week for four hours. Art instruction, recreation, swimming and a time of serious discussion are provided. The art instructor in 1966 was an art student at nearby Wesleyan College in Macon.

Youth Happening

Piano Drop: The Youth for Christ director in Philadelphia,

Bill Lewis, devised a special "Youth Happening" to assemble a crowd. He arranged for a section of South Philadelphia to be cleared off for a "Piano Drop." A helicopter was rented to drop the piano from a height of several hundred feet. Then the youth were given pieces of the piano as a souvenir. A time of Christian sharing followed the festive event.

Ecology Rock Festival: Jerry Edwards, formerly a Baptist minister in Chelsea, Massachusetts, tied in a ministry with the popular ecology concerns in 1970. He arranged to utilize a sports stadium for a rock festival. Edwards spread the word that the price of admission was a sack of garbage. The youth were instructed to pick up trash along the side of the streets and on vacant lots. Arrangements were made with the city for garbage trucks to collect and haul away the collection.

Many of the community youth had their first meaningful contact with the church through this effort. Through this initial meeting many of the young people began attending the coffeehouse at the Baptist Church in Chelsea.

Skating Party: The Oakhurst Baptist Church of Decatur, Georgia, initiated an every Saturday skating program for neighborhood youth. Young people in the church made the project possible with a $400 financial Christmas gift to buy 72 pair of skates.

The two hour program involves over 100 children. About two thirds of the youth had no previous contact with the church. Pastor John Nichol sees the skating ministry as the church's way of telling the community, "We are concerned for you as persons, and this is our way of serving you."

State Fair Performances: Churches and associations have effectively rented county and state fair booths for outreach ministries. The Delaware Valley Baptist association rented a booth at the 1969 New Jersey State Fair. They distributed free copies of the Good News Version of John. Church leaders were trained in counseling and Christian witnessing with interested visitors to the booth.

Other churches have shown the film, "Man In the Fifth Dimension." This was the Billy Graham Pavillion film at the New York World Fair. One church showed the film every hour on the hour at a tend at the Kentucky State Fair. An invitation for viewers to accept Christ was offered after every performance.

Diverse Worship Approaches

Beaches: Church of God pastor, Mark Forsyth, in Ventura, California, moved his Sunday services to the beach. He was convinced that the youth which the church needed to reach were at the beach. In eight years he has been the beach pastor to thousands of young people.

Reverend Forsyth communicates the Gospel effectively. The worship consists of hymns, Scripture reading, distribution of religious leaflets and shore-side preaching.

Race Tracks: The Gulfstream Race Track of Hallandale, Florida, is the site of a regular worship service during racing season. An area of the paint and sign shop was cleared and chairs were brought in. During the first racing session thirteen youth choirs came to the track to present their programs of testimony and music. The stable hands worship in their work clothes. Initially, some would sit outside in the darkness. Soon, the curiosity and refreshments broke down any resistance.

Parking Lot: Within a mile of America's key defense system, the Strategic Air Command Base in Bellevue, Nebraska, a series of outdoor worship services proved successful. The First Baptist Church held a J.O.Y. (Jesus, Other, You) Festival with music and brief messages. Over 50 young adults had some public commitment during three nights of activity.

Several years ago the youth choir from the Bethany Baptist Church of Dallas, Texas, assisted in an outdoor revival in Worcester, Mass. The choir presented a contemporary Gospel music presentation. This was followed by a brief message by the pastor of the Baptist church. Some 85 persons responded to an invitation to trust Christ during the week, and received counseling.

Golf Course: The Lahaina Baptist Mission on the Island of Maui in Hawaii has sponsored Easter services on the number nine green of the Kaanapali golf course. The service was held at 6 a.m. and drew over 800 in attendance.

Donald E. Davis of Sunrise Presbyterian Church in Miami, Florida, initiated a "sunrise eye-opener" worship service on Sunday at 8 a.m. at a country club for golfers. It was a combination breakfast and worship service. The average attendance each Sunday was 50 persons. His church membership has increased from 35 to 200 in two years.

Marketplace: The International Marketplace in Waikiki, Hawaii, becomes holy ground at 9 a.m. on Sunday. The Awikiki Mission of the Olivet Baptist Church conducts services for about 200 persons on an outdoor stage. Tourists dressed in bathing suits and other informal attire attend. As many as 150 persons participate in the mission, counting those who come for evening vespers. The ideas for the mission was a Billy Graham Crusade that was held in Hawaii in 1965.

Shopping Center: The Trinity Baptist Church of Lexington, Kentucky moved their Sunday evening services to a shopping center about a mile from the church for the summers of 1969 and 1970. An elevated walkway around the second floor provided a pulpit area. Six to seven hundred people attended each night. About one-third of that number were either unchurched or from other churches. All cars parked diagonally facing the loudspeakers. Deacons roving through the parking area provided a private enlistment for the Bible Fellowships at each car. The advertising campaign was "Come as you are — Sit in your car." Handbills, radio spot announcements and newspaper ads spread the word in the community. People making decisions for Christ turned on their car lights.

A flatbed truck becomes the platform from which the Walnut Street Baptist Church in Louisville, Kentucky, has held worship services. A youth rock band and scores of young people invade a shopping center to gather a crowd. They have a service of testimonies, music, and preaching.

The Beverly Hills Baptist Church of Asheville, N.C., which is at the gateway to the Smoky Mountains provided a ministry to reach the numerous tourists in the area. From early Spring to late Fall the twenty-five motels are filled with these visitors.

Pastor James L. Blevins began a "come-as-you-are" service in the parking lot of a nearby shopping center. The services were featured in advertisements at the motels. Also, church members went to strategic spots on Saturdays to give tourists personal invitations.

The thirty-minute services begin at 8:30 a.m. Travelers may then get an early start on their travels. The service includes a Sunday School lesson, musical selections from the youth choir and a brief sermon. There are an average of forty cars in attendance each week, with a maximum of 100 cars.

City Park: Parks worship services have been effective from Pennsylvania to Nebraska. One hundred sixty people accepted Christ in parks during the summer of 1970 in Johnstown, Pennsylvania. Worship services led by Reverend Jack Smith twice weekly reached hundreds of youth with contemporary Christian folk-rock selections. The youth group provided Christian counseling for those making public commitments during the services.

The youth group from the Westside Baptist Church of Omaha, Nebraska, sent a choir to the Sandhills city of Valentine. The group provided musical selections for park worship services. Hundreds of unchurched community youth had their first meaningful worship experience in a park. The informed music and messages reached about one hundred youth nightly for a week in a town of 2,800 people.

Drive-In Church: Creative pastors in California and Florida have delivered productive drive-in church ministries. The Pasadena Community Church of St. Petersburg, Florida, is officially connected with the Methodist Episcopal Church South. An amplifier was placed in the garden for the disabled in 1937. Rev. J. Wallace Hamilton was the famed pastor many years. In 1938 benches were provided on the church grounds for worship in an area now called Radio Park. Others sat in their cars to listen to the service. In 1940 the church leased other lots about the church to develop into a Radio Garden with a central address system. Today there are parking spaces and fine loudspeakers to assist 2,000 cars. The record attendance was Easter Sunday 1951 with 3,435 cars and 10,000 people.

Similarly, the Garden Grove Community Church of Garden Grove, California, is a Drive-In Church. Rev. Robert Schuller has pastored the church for nearly twenty years and it now has over 6,000 members. The church claims to be the largest walk-in, drive-in church in the world. Another million persons each week view the worship services on television, giving it the top regular religious viewing audience. An usher comes to car windows with a bulletin and instructs the worshipper to turn the car radio to 540 on the dial. Those without radios park on the back row and use the amplifiers. There are 1,700 seats in the sanctuary which are filled each Sunday.

Schuller emphasizes "the four principles of successful retailing: accessibility, surplus parking, inventory and service with a smile."[2] Sixty-five percent of all new members come on profession of faith in Christ for the first time. The church has also helped launch thirteen new congregations in California.

Drive-In Theater: Robert H. Schuller began his ministry in Orange County, California, in 1955. A drive-in theater was available and they initiated Sunday services there. A door-to-door canvas uncovered only two families of the Reformed

Church in America denomination. He began services at the Orange Drive-In on March 27 at 11 a.m. Advertisement urged people to "Come as you are in the family car." He used a small electric organ and was assisted by a neighboring choir. Fifty cars were present the first week. The pastor became known as the "Passion Pit Preacher." He preached from atop a snack bar for six years. The Garden Grove Community Church moved into a chapel three miles away after one and a half years. The church decided to continue the drive-in services at the theater also. Schuller had a dream of merging the chapel and drive-in congregation.

MOBILE MINISTRIES

America is the most mobile nation on earth. Personal automobiles have expanded man's lifestyle and broadened his horizons. The individual without an automobile is handicapped, as well as being a prisoner to time and chance.

Churches have responded with an increased sensitivity to the troubled masses for whom transportation is not readily available. They have developed a variety of helpful mobile ministries that fall in at least four categories — transporting, performing, delivering, and meeting sites.

In 1965 there were only twenty churches in the nation with as many as 200 conversions that were followed with believer's baptism. Twelve of those churches were Southern Baptist. Six years later in 1971, some 90 Southern Baptist congregations reported a similar achievement in a single year. Seventeen of these churches had baptized over 500 converts.

There is no single explanation for the intensive increase in evangelistic effectiveness. However, it is generally agreed that the use of church bus ministries has played a significant role in producing these results.

Mobile "Transporting" Ministries

Transporting To Church Services: Eugene Skelton in his book, *10 Fastest Growing Southern Baptist Sunday Schools*, has pinpointed seven characteristics of churches with growth through the use of buses: The churches have determined to reach people. They made proper advance preparation for the task. They enlisted an adequate number of workers and properly trained them. They enlarged the classes and departments in their Sunday School organization for the increased number before they began. They sent workers out every Saturday to visit the unchurched. They provided children's worship services to meet their needs. They majored on evangelism in the Bible study experience.

Churches utilizing the bus ministry are zealous in their efforts to reach beyond the walls of the church buildings for those who refuse to come to church. The general rule is that for every man-hour of visitation on a bus route, ten riders will board the bus on Sunday. Therefore, with four hours of Saturday visitation on a bus route, forty children should come Sunday. The church wanting to increase attendance by 400 persons would seek to send its buses on 40 routes each week.

Walker Knight commended the prospects of bold efforts in bus evangelism in *Home Missions* magazine. He assessed that it fills a vacuum in the life of the church. He also concluded that it gave the churches the opportunity to reach thousands who would be completely overlooked because of the indifference of their parents.

The First Baptist Church of Hammond, Indiana, probably has the most extensive bus ministry in the country with 108 buses transporting as many as 5,030 riders. The church budgets over $100,000 per year for bus evangelism. From these labors the church reaps the significant fruits of about 2,000 baptisms per year.

The Dauphin Way Baptist Church in Mobile, Alabama, is one of the most vigorous Southern Baptist churches in bus evangelism. Nearly half of all children attending the church's Sunday School come by bus. This is approximately 700 children each week.

Walker Knight provides a word of caution concerning bus evangelism. He warns that there is a danger of institutionalizing the bus ministry, in the same way that churches do this with their buildings.

Rev. Thomas Adams of the First Baptist Church of Des Plaines, Illinois, added other cautions in the October, 1975

Baptist Program. He indicated that his church voted to discontinue its bus ministry five years after it began. His results were quite good in the beginning, but a decline occurred. He reasoned that five years before, no other churches in the town had a bus ministry. The impact of First Baptist declined when others developed a bus ministry. He became bothered at the use of unethical gimmicks by some churches using this ministry. Finally, the zealous individuals who led in the ministry in the beginning moved. Then the nominating committee began having great difficulty in finding willing workers. The pastor concluded that a church should never keep a ministry just because everyone else is doing it.

The Church Services and Materials Division of the Sunday School Board has developed a wealth of resources to assist Baptist churches in their bus evangelism efforts. The key resource items include:

Outreach With Church Buses, compiled by Reginald McDonough

Children's Worship Book

Children's Worship Service Helps, edited by Mark Moore

Bus Outreach Starter Kit

Busing Ministry (cassette)

Outreach Through Bus Ministry (filmstrip)

Churches that blend caution with zeal have had exciting success in bus evangelism. Both small rural churches and large city churches testify to the effectiveness of buses as a tool to motivate members to have proper evangelistic concern.

Transporting People In a "Taxi" Ministry: Many people in low-income areas need transportation to everything from grocery stores to medical appointments. Churches with a random bus or taxicab service have met the physical, economic and emotional needs of troubled persons.

Greg Whitetree served as a Baptist US-2 volunteer in Honolulu, Hawaii. He operated a bus "taxicab" service in Hawaii for anyone needing a ride. He provided transportation for a blind woman and midnight emergency transportation to maternity hospitals as a means of ministry.

The Dinsmore Baptist Church of Jacksonville, Florida, has provided a bus transportation ministry to the physically handicapped. The service began with a van, but added space was soon necessary. The church bought a bus and stripped the inside to hold the wheelchairs. The chairs had to be belted down with the backs against the bus walls. A hydraulic lift was also purchased. Members of the church who were local mechanics helped with the labor.

This church ministry provides transportation to the church's Bethesda Club and also for trips to shopping centers.

Transporting on City Tours: The First Baptist Church of Charleston, S.C., has a bus tour of historic places to newcomers to the city. Reverend Paul Craven, the pastor, arranges for every new resident of the city to have an invitation to their city tour. All of the historic Civil War attractions are along the bus route. Members of the church mingle with their new neighbors during the trip. Other church members remain at the church to prepare a meal for the group after the tour.

Since the visitors have had a special treat and learned about the city, the pastor informs them of the ministries at First Baptist Church.

This procedure has been successful in cultivating many new citizens for evangelistic results.

Similarly, the Dinsmore Baptist Church of Jacksonville provides the handicapped with trips to the airport, museums and the zoo, as well as athletic events.

Transporting Parade Float Ministry: There are mobile ministries that don't use buses. Former Southern Baptist Convention President, Rev. Wayne Dehoney says that parades are "one of the great means of witnessing in South America, as we discovered in the Crusade of the Americas. They are also effective in North America. An increasing number of churches are entering floats in city parades, as a means of ministry and community involvement.

Three Baptist churches in Nebraska made strong inroads with the people of their communities with parade floats. The Calvary Baptist Church of Sidney had a float that won first place in the city's "Happiness" Parade. The theme of the Baptist float was "Happiness is Believing God's Promise."

The Faith Baptist Church of Nebraska City entered a float in the nationally famous Arbor Day Parade on April 23, 1972. This has been a church ministry for several years that has kept the church's ministry in the minds of the city people. Similarly, the Bethel Baptist Church of Scottsbluff finished in third place with a float in the Oregon Trail Days Parade. This honor resulted in a front page newspaper story, accompanied by the pastor's picture.

Mobile "Performing"

Puppet Show: The First Baptist Church of Lemon Grove, California, has a puppet show connected with their bus ministry. Rev. Bob Kleinschmidt is pastor of this church, which makes and sells puppets. Workers in other churches are trained by the puppet-ministry leaders in performing this ministry.

The puppet shows are held on buses and in backyards. Members distribute leaflets throughout the community to draw a crowd. The shows are usually provided every Thursday afternoon during the summer.

"This community was a graveyard for preachers for the last eight years," reports missionary Wayne Burlick. This ministry helped the church grow from 150 to 600 members.

The church also has a famous singing group which goes on tours — The Californians. The group was on the variety show in the summer of 1970 which filled in for the Carol Burnett Show.

Ventriloquism and Movies: Reverend and Mrs. Meredith Wyatt lead a Baptist associational ministry in the summers in

Bakersfield, California. Mrs. Wyatt performs with a ventriloquist to entertain the children. The couple show Campus Crusade magic movies and Moody Science films at shopping centers and county fairs. The couple has taken the ministry from the black and Mexican poverty areas to fashionable ski resorts. In addition to the entertainment, they teach the children Scripture and songs about Jesus.

Reverend Wyatt frequently drives up in front of someone's home for a lawn party. Forty or fifty children will get on the bus for the presentation. The minister took the mobile chapel to the County Fair and reached 1019 people in nine days. The ministry resulted in 64 conversions to Christ. Baptist church leaders assisted in the ministry by serving coffee and providing hospitality.

The mobile chapel also contains a cassette tape library. Wyatt's teaching ministry reaches an average of 184 persons a week, throughout the year.

The Dinsmore Baptist Church of Jacksonville, Florida, takes a weekday arts and crafts program into trailer parks, dairy farms and isolated sections of the community. Church leaders show movies and tell Bible stories. The programs last about two hours. There are several stations where these ministries are performed, and the activities are held at each station once a week.

Gingerbread House: A children's chapel, known as the "Gingerbread House" was designed by the Child Evangelism Fellowship leaders in Richmond, California, to reach unchurched children. It allowed the leaders to penetrate an area where it was "almost impossible to get work started."

The mobile trailer, decorated like a "Gingerbread House" was the site of 1,000 decisions for Christ. The 19 x 8 foot unit has redwood siding and seats 42. The chapel contains a projector shelf and screen for showing films. It is pulled easily by any car.

The Richmond Child Evangelism Fellowship has been asked

to bring the chapel to shopping centers to tell stories to the children, according to Director Doris McMullen.

Mobile "Delivering" Ministries

Books: A bookmobile as a form of mobile ministry is referred to in the seventh chapter of this book. Reverend Floyd Tidsworth, former pastor in Wheeling, West Virginia, has reached unchurched youth and adults in previously unpenetrated areas through a bus bookmobile. The project also served as a means of church extension for developing new missions.

Recreation: Reverend Elvis Markham, pastor of the Graceland Baptist Church of New Albany, Indiana, uses a bus to deliver recreational equipment to youth at parks. The youth are directed in baseball games and other events by church staff members. The bus transports balls, bats and other needed equipment.

Medical Help: Innovative churches have used buses to bring Christian care for the physical needs of the community. Walker Knight in *Home Missions Magazine* wrote about the diversity of bus usage by churches. ' Another became a clinic to help meet health needs." Such a ministry in low income communities may provide the only health care and immunization some people ever receive.

Mobile Facility As a "Meeting Place

Branch Sunday Schools: The Graceland Baptist Church of New Albany, Indiana, utilizes 14 buses for branch Sunday Schools. The buses go to unchurched children and teach them the Sunday School lesson in their own community. This provides the opportunity to cultivate an area for the formation of a new mission. The Walnut Street Baptist Church of Louisville has also provided trailers for Sunday.

Youth Bible Fellowship Study: The Woodlawn Baptist Church of Decatur, Georgia, sends buses each weekday to three city high schools to involve students in Bible study. Students at the Towers and Columbia high schools meet the bus each morning at 7:30 a.m. All of the seats have been cleared out of the bus and the floors have been carpeted. The church leaders assist the youth in Bible study and prayer until class time.

Trailer Park Activities: The Walnut Street Baptist Church of Louisville, Kentucky, has placed a trailer in the middle of a mobile park. It has used the facility in weekday nursery school and childcare programs. The church lay leaders have also led Wednesday night prayer services. Park owners often donate space to a church. The income from the day nursery offsets the cost of the program and the trailer payments.

Anti-Occult Mobile Unit : Evangelist Morris Cerullo began a tour of 45 American cities in the summer of 1972 with an Anti-Occult mobile unit. He filled a trailer with 100 items associated with the occult and magic to educate teenagers about witchcraft and satanism. The Black Mass, sorcery and blood-drinking orgies are other aspects of the occult that Cerullo exhibited.

Cerullo, founder and president of the World Evangelism, Inc., says the mobile unit is designed to turn people away from diabolism. His staff made a $30,000 six month study of the occult. They discovered that 10 million Americans dauble in the occult and 100,000 more worship the devil.

The "witchmobile" displays potions, voodoo oils, a satanic altar, and a goat's hoof. The mobile unit is staffed by members of the San Bernadino Teen Power evangelistic group.

Worship Facility: Transport for Christ is a Christian organization to assist truck drivers with nine fulltime chaplains, 37 truck-evangelists and 70 associates. They seek to counsel troubled truckers and comfort the families of drivers who have died in accidents. The International Headquarters are located in Waterdown, Ontario.

In 1968 the organization purchased a 40 foot ' Trailblazer"

mobile chapel for worship services. They also publish a tabloid paper, *The Highway Evangelist*.

The Trailblazer has traveled over 100,000 miles in 43 states and eight provinces. James Keys, the founder and director, was a truck driver when he was converted. He began the organization with a concern for the families of the 33 drivers who die on American and Canadian highways every week.

Similarly, the mobile chapel that Rev. Bill Frazier uses at the NASCAR races was mentioned previously in the book. In three years his trailer services have grown from seven drivers to one audience of 70,000 racing spectators. Driver Richard Petty, top NASCAR winner, has been a supporter of this ministry.

Counseling Service: Alcoholism is one of the chief problems in the industry. Industrial chaplains spend much time in marital counseling and family problems. About 80 to 90 percent of all industrial accidents stem from emotional stress and disorders according to medical consultants.

Counseling has become a major need for truckers in addition to providing worship services. The chaplain may be a vital link between the worker and the church. For many workers the chaplain is the only tie with Christian values and beliefs.

The opportunities for using motor vehicles in the proclamation of Jesus Christ are endless. Through the use of a bus or automobile a church may be able to befriend a rebellious youth or comfort a distressed senior citizen. These vehicles may serve as the stage for providing individuals the occasion to worship God in locations far from church buildings. Children, youth and adults without facilities to travel to church services may discover new hope in Christ because a church chose to send a bus through their neighborhood.

The full potential for the utilization of mobile transportation for the glory of God has not been tapped. However, the Spirit of God will enable the Christian who sincerely searches for ways to share the caring concern of Christ, to do so. In future generations churches will search for the implications of helicopters, airplanes, spaceships and lunar land transportation as means of proclaiming to the universe that God was in Christ, reconciling the world unto himself.

NON-PERSONAL CONFRONTATIONS (ELECTRONICS)

Electronics

Radio: A noted radio evangelist has estimated that by investing $100 in radio and television time he can reach 300,000 with a gospel presentation. He concludes that the entire population of the world could be reached if 13,333 persons each gave $100. Four billion persons would be confronted with the gospel for $1.3 million.

This estimate may not be realistic or possible, but it stresses the impact of the electronic media.

Where does a church get started? Clarence E. Duncan, assistant to the Director of the Southern Baptist Convention Radio and Television Commission has suggested guidelines for a church to have success on television:

> General information about a station should be secured before the first contact (frequency or channel, power, coverage, networks, etc.)
>
> The station and its programs should be viewed and heard first in order to know what you are talking about when you call.
>
> Make an appointment with the program director to discover whether public service time is available, and if so, the types of programming offered.
>
> Answer the following questions: What is your message? Do you know the basic ideas you want to get across? What is the best way to put your message across?
>
> Submit specific facts and workable concepts.[1]

Many stations have a policy against soliciting funds. The church should discover the station's policy before asking for financial assistance.

Any interviews with the station management should be by appointment. All on-the-air commitments must be honored with promptness.

A typewritten copy of the program should be submitted to the program director a week to ten days in advance of air time. The copy should be triple-spaced on 8 1/2 by 11 paper.

At the top of each page, list the church's name, address and telephone number. The copy material should be timed at a slightly faster pace for radio than television.

A slide is preferable as a television visual aid over a photograph. One picture should be provided for each ten seconds on the air.

There are a variety of formats from which a church has to choose in initiating a communication ministry:

Religious News: Religious news involves church related activities that seek to improve the spiritual or social conditions in a given community. Local religious events can be discovered through ministerial associations. This allows religious news broadcasts to include "exclusives."

National and international religious news can be acquired from these sources:

Religious News Service, 43 West 57th Street, New York, N.Y.

Church Broadcasting Associates, P.O. Box 186, San Anselmo, California.

Local Radio Wire Services

Denominational and Interdenominational agencies.

Throughout the country many Southern Baptist churches conduct religious news programs. Some concentrate on Southern Baptist news, but most have realized that the listening audience increases when news cuts across community and denominational lines.

First Baptist Church, Carmi, Illinois, had a five minute newscast on Sundays at 8:30 a.m. They promoted the general work of the church and the Crusade of the Americas.

The Southern Baptist Convention Radio and Television Commission has assisted production of five-minute religious news programs on more than 380 radio stations in thirteen states.

Don Sturgis, the Commission's Director of News, produces the newscasts. The programs are then mailed within hours to the stations for broadcasting as a public service news feature. The news content varies in each state.

Clarence E. Duncan, executive assistant of the Radio and Television Commission says,

> Each news cast has at least one thing in common. It attempts to bring people up to date on happenings within their church communities and to inform them about the work of groups of other religious faiths in their states.[2]

The Hour of Decision (a half hour of time, the word "Hour" in the title following the normal custom of American radio) went out over 150 stations on ABC network on Sunday, November 5, 1950 from Georgia. They received 178,726 letters the first year and 362,595 in 1952.

The Radio and Television Commission is available to assist in the preparation of news programs for individual churches or associations of churches. It will also suggest time clearance and audience building techniques.

Devotionals: Most radio devotional programs are of a poor quality. Men who are deliberately careful in pulpit presentations often poorly prepare a message for a devotional broadcast.

Any religious program competes for listeners with professional, commercial productions. Dr. Peter Eldersveld, well known preacher on the "Back to God Hour" spent four hours rehearsing on a fifteen minute broadcast in advance of the actual broadcast.

Evangelism can be inserted into a devotional message by stressing the way one assumes the responsibilities of the

Christian life. A series of three months duration needs a theme.

Simple language is preferable to theological cliches. The message is more effective if written out. Music selections should be brief hymns of a stately, majestic nature for maximum impact. The basic rule is for the music to be complementary to the message.

The radio listener is generally an audience of one person—housewife, automobile driver or shut-in. Speak to this audience of one personally and confidentially. Courage must be communicated to the weary. The Bible should be presented as hope to the guilty or distressed.

Many stations may be open to brief devotional messages at sign-on and sign-off time. Audiences are smaller at these hours but good publicity methods can increase the viewing audience.

The Baptist Hour, a thirty minute, professionally-produced program, is heard on nearly 400 stations each week. Over 5,600 letters a year are written in response to the program. It is composed of sixteen minutes of inspirational hymns and gospel songs, followed by a forceful thirteen minute devotional message.

Churches can help secure the broadcast on an appropriate local radio station that reaches a general audience of all ages.

No fees are charged to the radio station by the Radio and Television Commission for the use of the program. In return, the station provides public service time free for the broadcast of "The Baptist Hour" or a variety of other Southern Baptist broadcasts.

The procedure for securing the program involves:

Request an audition tape from the Radio and Television Commission.

Call the station and ask for an appointment to talk with the manager or program director.

Praise the manager for his responsible broadcasting and express appreciation for his efforts in community betterment.

Show him the audition tape and ask if he would listen to it with you.

Emphasize: (a) The Baptist Hour is carried on 450 stations. (b) Baptists across the country seek to promote the program. (c) Explain that for over thirty years the professionally produced program has been non-denominational and inoffensive to other groups. (d) Ask if he would use it on a regular basis on public service time. (e) Explain your association of churches will help build an audience for "The Baptist Hour."

Ask the manager or Program Director to notify the marketing services of the Radio and Television Commission and express desire to begin.

Notify broadcaster of other Radio and Television Commission programs without cost.[3]

In 1950, Fred Dienert of the Walter Bennett Advertising Company told Billy Graham, "That a peak Sunday afternoon time would shortly be available coast-to-coast on the American Broadcasting Company's network, for an initial thirteen week's contract at a total of $92,000.00.[4] Graham began his radio ministry with this $7,000 per week rate and has continued for twenty-two years. It went out over 150 stations on ABC network on November 5, 1950.

The National Association of Broadcasters, composed of representatives of 3,300 radio and 522 television stations, voted Graham the 1972 Distinguished Service Award. This was the "radio and television industry's highest honor" and acknowledged the superb quality of the program.

Worship: The largest Baptist church in the world, First Baptist of Dallas, televises two worship services each Sunday. However, they broadcast the third worship service over the radio. The pastor of the church with the alleged world's largest Sunday School has a daily radio worship broadcast on nearly 100 stations. The program, "Old Time Gospel Hour" is broadcasted by the Rev. Jerry Falwell, pastor of the Independent Thomas Road Baptist Church in Lynchburg, Virginia.

Time and thought, prayer and planning should be vital ingredients in broadcasting a worship service. It is an awesome task to fill a one hour time period. Someone has said that prayer without planning is impotent. Likewise, planning without prayer is impoverishing.

Music clearance sheets containing titles, names of authors and publishing companies should be submitted several days in advance of the broadcast for proper clearance.

The radio audience is not a "captive audience." He may turn his set off or change stations without embarrassment. It is helpful to tighten up slack so that it flows smoothly.

There are two alternatives for beginning the broadcast. The choir may sing a call to worship or the congregation could be singing a lively hymn. An anthem by the choir is an effective way to meaningfully fill the offertory period. The minister could use this time to speak directly to the radio audience. The minister must watch the clock if the invitation is included in the broadcast.

Spot Announcements: Following a fast and frantic recorded music radio presentation, a layman's confident voice identified himself and offered his Christian witness. He asked, "Are you a family man?" He then told of his proud family. He informed listeners of another family to which he belonged — God's.

Immediately the next record on the music survey began. Nine deacons from First Baptist Church, Fairfax, South Carolina were engaged in this spot radio evangelism campaign. Each man explained his salvation experience in understandable and simple terms.

No reference in the broadcast was made to the church's facilities or organizations. The church bought ninety spots on three radio stations in the area. Ten spots were broadcast

Thursday through Saturday.

Forty-one radio spot packages have been produced for local churches by Timerite, Inc., a division of the Southern Baptist Convention Radio and Television Commission, for $100. All 41 spots are open end for local identification, such as church name and address. This combination may be divided into four sets: (a) Eleven 30 second spots; (b) Ten 30 second revival spots; (c) Ten 60 second general; (d) Ten 30 second general.

A spot may convey a devotional thought with greater force and clarity than a longer message.

The First Baptist Church, Jonesboro, Illinois, has used a one-minute commercial in the daily broadcast that the church sponsors to comment on some phase of world or local news and to make a spiritual application.

The spot is now recognized as a significant form of religious broadcasting. A ten second spot can often accomplish more than a fifteen minute program. Ten seconds can carry twenty-five words, such as "Long ago someone said, 'How lovely are the faces of those who talk with God.' Prayer is part of every service at Bethany Baptist Church."

Spot radio will be heard. No listener will bother to turn off a minute spot, even if he'd refuse to hear a brief devotional.

Panel Discussion: There is a reservoir of popular religious subjects to provide a basis for a religious panel show that would be of interest to non-Christians.

A starting point is to secure a moderator who will control the panel members. His personality gives continuity to the program. Monotonous monologues with religious cliches should be avoided. "Should your conscience be your guide?" Or "How does religion relate to one's business or social life?" are stimulating subjects.

Pre-broadcast rehearsals are to be discouraged. The panel will find it difficult to remember which comments were made on the air, and which were stated in the practice run.

Music Presentations: Several professionally produced programs should have widespread interest to churches. Southern Baptists produce a thirty minute weekly program of country music and interviews with recording stars. It is entitled, "Country Crossroads" and is on 534 stations. In 1971 there were 30,131 letters in response — many of which were counseling letters.

Another thirty minute program geared for teens on 632 stations is "Powerline." It majors of "Top 40" type music, problem mail session and comments of contemporary life. Over 8,500 people a year respond to this program with mail.

"Master Control" which is heard on 625 stations is 30-minute weekly variety program with popular music and general interest interviews. In 1971 there were 6,282 letters written to the Radio and Television Commission in response to these shows.

When locally produced, the music program must have a purpose. This makes it easier to plan a program. In planning any musical program the selections to be used should be submitted to the station in time for clearance.

Interviews: A Baptist pastor in Plattsmouth, Nebraska, secured a ten minute interview for his guest evangelist. The interviewer was assisted by calls from the radio audience. The evangelist displayed remarkable knowledge of all denominations and was articulate in answering questions on abortion, homosexuality, the generation gap and other popular subjects. The announcer was so impressed that the interview was extended to fifty-five minutes.

Good interviews result from adequate experience on the part of the interviewer and an interesting subject.

Questions calling for a "yes" or "no" answer should be avoided. The interviewer's informality will relax the situation.

Theodore Lott lists five interview categories: (a) Unusual hobbies; (b) Important occupations; (c) Novel undertakings;

(d) Celebrities; (e) Personal Christian testimonies.

Television

Evangelist Oral Roberts ended his tent ministry in 1968 to enter the mass media ministry. Roberts said he saw the tent would no longer get the job done so he'd rather be in the home, and he could do that with TV. Today Oral Roberts evangelizes with TV specials costing a half million dollars.

The young Texas evangelist James Robison has launched a prime-time national series featuring the best Christian talent from across the country.

Variety Programs: "Spring Street, U.S.A." premiered February 11, 1973, on 20 TV stations, as the first Southern Baptist presentation of the gospel with a variety show format. The half-hour program began with a 13-week series. Twenty-one episodes were filmed by January 1, 1974.

Dr. Kenneth Chafin, a Houston pastor, said that the show attempts to communicate Jesus Christ and invite men to a personal relationship with him through music, interviews and a message.

Dr. Fred Mosley of the Home Mission Board encouraged Baptists who would like for the program to be broadcast in their area, and who would provide financial support toward purchase of time to contact the Board.

Spot Announcements: The 1972 Nebraska-Colorado football game had an enormous viewing audience on network television. The Evangelical Free Church of Nebraska purchased an effective one-minute spot announcement during the game for the Nebraska viewing audience. The head football coach at Columbus High School in Columbus, Nebraska, utilized the entire minute. He gave a personal testimony of his conversion experience with Jesus Christ. His message was seen by thousands more than any Sunday half-hour religious program.

Dramatic Presentations: "My greatest opportunity for witness comes through my television ministry," Philadelphia minister Harry Bristow states. Bristow sponsors the religious movie or dramatic TV program known as "Christian Cinema." "We have the top rating of the three Philadelphia UHF stations when we're on the air," Bristow emphasized.

Christian Cinema has been on Channel 29 for over ten years. Funds to finance the program are solicited through the mail, as on-the-air appeals are prohibited.

The effects of the television series are far-reaching. The head of the New Jersey Mafia told Bristow that he regularly watches the television show in his night club.

Southern Baptists produce a thirty minute dramatic TV program entitled "The Answer," which is seen on about 75 stations. It is a series of inspirational dramas dealing with Biblical themes and current issues.

Cartoons: Twenty-thousand dollars is spent by Southern Baptists for each episode of the four and one-half minute cartoon called JOT, which is on 76 stations. This little character was created by the Radio and Television Commission. JOT depicts real-life situations for boys and girls between ages five and eleven. The cartoons portray the importance of harmony with both God and man. Hundreds of thousands of children across the nation are reached with Bible verses.

The First Baptist Church of Tallahassee, Florida, aired JOT on Sunday mornings during their televised worship service for eight weeks in 1972. At the conclusion of each JOT program, an invitation was given to attend Vacation Bible School. The Marketing Department of the Radio and Television Commission will prepare such arrangements for interested churches.

One-Minute Sermons: Unchurched residents of Pensacola, Florida, are being reached in an innovative way. Rev. James L. Pleitz, pastor of the First Baptist Church began effectively using spot announcements in 1969. The spots are produced by the Southern Baptist Convention Radio and Television

Commission and shown twice daily by a Pensacola station.

Pleitz says, "You know, as some doors are closed because of changing times and conditions, it seems that other doors open. There are many high-rise apartments...and our church visitors can't get past the locked lobby to visit with the good news of the gospel."

Some of these one-minute sermons will be released to stations in the top 100 markets across the nation with a potential listening audience of 100 million people.

Pleitz is filmed in a variety of non-church settings. He is seen at a golf course, at the beach, in his backyard and at a park pitching a baseball with a child.

In some spots Pleitz urges the listeners to play catch with God in a lifetime partnership. In other spot announcements he reminds that God can cleanse lives from the rust and damage of sin.

He maintains that if he had to make a choice between preaching one hour on Sunday morning or one minute on radio or television, he'd choose the one minute spots.

Worship Services: Independent Baptist pastor Jerry Falwell produces a half-hour worship service on TV known as the "Old Time Gospel Hour." The program is seen on over 400 stations across the nation.

The North Phoenix Baptist Church of Phoenix, Arizona, broadcasts their worship service in three states. The final five minutes of the program are filmed in advance and devoted to a special appeal to the TV audience. The church's telephone number is imposed on the screen, and four men sit by the phones to counsel callers. During a two year period 25 percent of the church's new members came as a result of the broadcast.

The vastness of television's potential viewing audience for worship is seen in the 35 million who watched the three hour long TV specials about EXPLO '72. This TV series was sponsored by Campus Crusade for Christ concerning the Dallas meetings and cost a million dollars to produce.

Secular Talk Shows: Billy Graham has preached to millions of unbelievers through the television medium of the secular talk show. Jack Parr, Joey Bishop, Johnny Carson, Dick Cavett and David Frost have all given Graham strategic access to the viewing audience which is largely unchurched.

Evangelist Bob Harrington gained prominence with network exposure on the Art Linkletter show. He impressed Linkletter's staff that he had something of interest to offer the sixteen million viewers of Houseparty in June, 1966.

Since then, Harrington has appeared on the Phil Donahue Show which originated on WLWD in Dayton, Ohio. He confronted atheist Madalyn Murray O'Hair several times on that show. He also appeared on the old Joe Pyne Show which formerly originated in Hollywood.

Motion Pictures

Motion picture films have a phenomenal potential for good or evil. The advertisement pages of the newspaper emphasize the latter. A variety of Christian experiments give evidence of the former usage. There are four ways that the Billy Graham Evangelistic Association has utilized films productively and redemptively.

Films for Occasional Church Showings: During the early 1950's the Billy Graham Evangelistic Association entered motion picture production. It is now estimated that every 35 minutes a Billy Graham film is showing somewhere in the world. Religious movies are made for individual local church showings on a rental basis. "Mr. Texas" and "The Heart Is A Rebel" were two of the successful efforts presenting the Gospel through film. Most major Christian denominations have similar dramatic movie productions.

Film Revivals: In recent years representations of the Evangelistic Association have provided a week of revival services using religious motion pictures. The representative sets the spiritual atmosphere in the service and offers a personal plea during the invitation hymn for unbelievers to accept Christ. A different film is used each night of the week. Widespread newspaper and community publicity is geared for reaching the general public.

Films at Fair Pavillions: The New York World's Fair in 1964-65 provided a setting for another Billy Graham Gospel confrontation by film. The central feature of the Graham Pavillion was a twenty-eight minute film, "Man In the Fifth Dimension." At each showing of the picture, Billy Graham gave an invitation on film for people to accept Christ.

Films in Theaters and Auditoriums: With the decade of the sixties, the Graham organization began producing top quality, feature-length movies for distribution in rented theaters. The audience paid an admission price to see the picture. "Christians buy tickets and bring their friends and pray for their friends,"[5] was one report.

"The Restless Ones" dealt with problems facing modern youth and was linked to Graham's Los Angeles Crusade. The successful effort included a time of public commitment to Christ at the end of the movie. Local ministers and church leaders had been previously trained as counselors for the venture. Nine and a half million people saw "The Restless Ones" during the first four years. There were 400,000 public commitments for Christ at the theaters during that period.

"For Pete's Sake" and "Two A Penny" are more recent productions by the World Wide Pictures distributors. "Two A Penny," the Cliff Richard's flim, is "the biggest production to date" for the company, and is considered an unusually powerful piece of evangelism.

The American Baptist Convention has entered the commercial film distributing business in a manner similar to the Graham approach. The denominations venture, Gateway Films, booked the religious movie, "The Cross and the

Switchblade," in about 300 theaters across the nation. They also released "The Late Liz," the Gert Behanna biography which starred Academy Award winners Anne Baxter and Jack Albertson. Gateway films planned to release many other films with a religious message.

Christian Films In Christian-Owned Theaters: Harry Bristow began Christian Cinema in a commercial motion picture theater in Philadelphia in 1948. A non-profit corporation bought the property. The Cinema has relocated in the suburbs.

"There's never a movie showing without someone being saved," Bristow states. They had two showings each week and offered a hymn of invitation after each.

"Thousands have been saved there through the years," Bristow adds. "It would be impossible to know exactly how many."

"We bought a theater because we knew that non-Christians would come there to witness the Christian dramas. Later we changed the name to "Cinema 33" to have a draw for more unbelievers. The title "33" refers to the age at which Christ died. So many theaters are called Cinema I or II that the name doesn't frighten people away."

The theater had 700 seats. The ministry was recently detoured in preparation for the next stage.

The movies were shown at the Huntingdon Valley Presbyterian Church while the new theater was being completed. This site eliminated many non-Christians from attending. But some always attended.

Christian Cinema has moved about sixteen miles north of Glenside into a new multi-purpose Christian complex. There is a theater with 600 seats, a bowling alley, a swimming pool and an ice skating rink. Christians work in all phases of the complex and bear a witness to the public about Christ.

Secular Films in Theaters: Robert Konzelman has suggested beneficial uses of secular films by the church. His book, *Marquee Ministries, The Movie Theater As Church and Community Forum*, emphasizes the influence of all cultural surroundings in our lives.

With the average feature film costing $3.3 million, he emphasizes we cannot belittle the secular motion picture and its influence out of our culture by ignoring it. Twenty million American people buy tickets to the movies each week, and only about four out of ten are above twenty-five years of age.

The impact of pictures is compounded by re-runs of older films on television. When Ben-Hur was broadcast, 86 million viewers say it on one night.

"Of the approximately three hundred (films) offered to the American public each year, perhaps less than twenty percent could be regarded in any way potentially useful to the church," Konzelman suggested.

He said that entire congregations might be encouraged to attend an inspirational movie like "Cromwell." One of two approaches is suggested for the conclusion at the film. First, the church may make arrangements with the theater management to conduct a public discussion at this special showing. An alternative procedure would be for the congregation to be directed to specific homes for small group discussions.

This use of movies, because of a neutral setting, has a potential attraction for involving unchurched persons in a confrontation in spiritual matters. With 14,000 motion picture theaters operating in the United States, (9,500 indoor and 4,500 outdoor drive-ins) the forum settings for proclaiming the Gospel are significantly increased.

Theaters have also been utilized for worship without films. The use of both indoor and outdoor theaters as a setting for preaching services is discussed in Chapter Four.

Computers

Rev. Tom Pendergrass, minister at the Bayside Baptist Church of Virginia Beach, Virginia, says, he believes a computer can be, for many churches a valuable tool for serving the church and community.

"The Billy Graham Association has no alternative between automation and chaos; for instance, over 75,000 change of addresses are reported to Minneapolis every month,"[6] states a reporter. "At present a General Electric 425 Computer is the mainstay, programmed for some three hundred different activities,"[7] the Association contends.

There are two practical services of a computer in evangelistic church outreach.

Geographical Matching For Visitation: Once the digited computer has been programmed for each member, the information is contained on a card with eighty separate digits. Rev. Pendergrass says, "The best way to visualize it is to imagine a row of eighty blanks which are to be filled in with a letter or a number."[8]

There are 1200 members of the Bayside Church congregation. "It took less than two minutes for the actual printing of all the information on each of the cards,"[9] according to the pastor.

A list of all Sunday School members above age nine, who are not church members, can be arranged by sub-division within minutes. This allows visitation to be expedient and efficient.

The Virginia pastor testifies, "The computer's versatility is limited only by the imagination of the church staff and the programmer."[10]

The First Baptist Church of Dallas, Texas, also uses a computer. Any new family moving to Dallas is in one of the church's 600 city zones, two miles square. Each of the 15,000 members are arranged in a zone, too. There are 150 witnessing teams of four men each, responsible for each zone. A staff member says, "Whenever a new family moves into any area of Dallas, that family will receive a witness of Christ from one of the 600 team members."[11]

Interest Matching For Visitation: "The computerized membership files will enable us to organize our evangelistic outreach in an effective way,"[12] says James W. Bryant of the First Baptist Church staff in Dallas. He also indicated that plans were being made with the Membership Services, Inc. computer service to compute the prospect files. The computer would help match the background profile of a member with an unchurched person they might reach for Christ.

The prospect may be 31 years old, and an insurance junior executive who lives in North Dallas. Perhaps he moved from Houston, plays golf and has a son in junior high school. The computer could locate an active member most like the prospect.

"This would be 'computerized evangelism,' the first century message being propagated through a twentieth-century method,"[13] Bryant said.

Cassette Tape Recorder

The church claiming the fastest growing Sunday School in America is the Independent Thomas Road Baptist in Lynchburg, Virginia. Every service at the church is taped on a cassette recorder. These tapes are sold to shut-ins in convalescent homes, servicemen or college students. This is viewed as a form of saturation evangelism.

The Polytechnic Baptist Church in Ft. Worth, Texas, has a similar ministry. They have initiated a Cassette Sunday School Department.

In order to minister to about 45 home bound members, the church purchased 25 cassette tape players. They bought them for less than $20.00 each. The church then secured 75 cassette tapes with a lifetime guarantee. This meant that with three tapes for each player, the church would have no more expenses.

The shut-ins had obvious, personal, spiritual and mental needs. The pastor taught the lessons on the recording. Several firms agreed to duplicate the master tape each week and the church selected a director to involve people in delivering the tapes. These people would visit the shut-ins, bringing new tapes each week and returning the used ones to the church.

Inter-Communications System

Progressive schools throughout the country use the school-home phone concept of providing a speaker and receiver in the classroom. Another receiver is put in the homes of sick students so they may keep up with daily school work in their absence.

The Selma Baptist Church in Johnston Association, North Carolina, initiated a similar ministry known as "Tel-In."

Shut-ins now participate in worship services, prayer meetings and revivals of the church. The church has nine "Tel-In" units in the homes of disabled people with another unit on the pulpit. The units are connected by telephone lines that provide perfect reception.

The system for the nine homes and the church was $170. Following this installation fee there is a cost of $182.50 per month for each unit. There is also a fee of $1.50 for each one-fourth mile. The pastor, Rev. D. Wayne Martin, says, "the families of the shut-ins are paying the monthly cost to the church which is billed by the telephone company."[14]

Electronic evangelism, group therapy, Bible study, fellowship, prayer, worship — any of these titles describe the nature of their ministry.

NON-PERSONAL CONFRONTATIONS (LITERATURE)

A mass media evangelistic or church growth campaign is the most effective way to reach the maximum number of people with the message of Christ's redemption. A mass media effort uses one or more communication vehicles such as newspapers, magazines, radio, television and direct mail. The potential of such media efforts still has not been developed to its capacity.

The vehicles of mass media evangelism may be divided into two key categories — literature and electronic. Both categories involve non-personal presentations of the Gospel. While all successful ministries would acknowledge that person-to-person, one-to-one encounters are preferable, the results of mass media evangelism are impressive.

Literature

Newspapers: Nearly 62 million English speaking newspapers are purchased every day in the United States. The English language newspapers in this country include 323 morning editions and 1,367 evening publications. These 1700 newspapers sell a combined total of 61,868,680 copies. In any given city the circulation will fluctuate between several thousand readers of a small town paper to over two million readers of the *New York News*.

Carl F. Henry, long-time publisher of *Christianity Today* once estimated that during World War II there were 35 million appreciative readers of Christian literature. He concluded that 25 percent or nine million people who are not church attenders read the literature. This indicated the enormous power of the press to reach people with Christian truth who never hear the Gospel otherwise.

Consider the possibilities. Christian churches have utilized a diversity of successful techniques in newspaper communication to help achieve church growth.

Advertisements

Hershey Candy, Wrigley Spearmint Gum, Coca-Cola and Volkswagen cars have one thing in common — they believe in advertising. They spend millions of dollars a year promoting their products.

The church seeking to reach people through newspaper advertising must make a decision. Suppose a congregation has budgeted $50 a month for reaching newspaper readers. It must decide whether to spend it all one week with a large ad or purchase four smaller weekly ads.

One choice may be to take one ad four columns wide by six inches length. This single appearance might reach 50,000 readers. However, for the same cost a church could buy four issues of an ad one column by six inches. The readership potential increases four-fold to 200,000.

Most churches purchase an ad concerning their worship services in the Saturday religious section of the paper. This generally lists the church's name and address, as well as times of worship services and sermon topic. Christian newcomers to a community might respond to this approach but few unbelievers will.

The Omaha Church of Christ has an interesting advertising effort. The church bought space in a neighborhood paper two columns by five inches. The name, address and telephone number of the church were listed at the top. Then there was a bold headline, "Who is a Christian?" There was an answer of 180 words — ten words per line for eighteen lines. The final phrase in bold type read, "Remember, The Bible is Right."

An Experimental advertisement effort by Southern Baptist

in Philadelphia had interesting results. An ad two columns by three inches read, "Guilty? Lonely? Afraid? Depressed? Life Can Begin Again! For Professional Counsel, Write, Counselor, P.O. Box 1140, Philadelphia, Pa., 19136." The two most interesting replies came from a Catholic priest and a woman friend. Curiously, both letters had been typed on the same typewriter and were enclosed in similar plain envelopes. Their responses were cries for help from troubled and related individuals.

A series of ads appeared in the Personal column of the classified ads of the three Philadelphia daily papers. The ad was only five or six lines in length. It read, "Do you have problems and don't know where to turn for help? For minister's counsel, call Ho 4-9708, Tuesdays and Fridays between 10:00 A.M. and 4:00 P.M." Hundreds of persons responded to the ad during the nine month telephone ministry.

News Stories: Newspaper editors are concerned about church activities which would be of interest to the community in general. For a staff member to get maximum news coverage, several guidelines are helpful. First, stories of an unusual nature, particularly with reference to children, have real possibilities. Second, regular communication with a single individual at the newspaper is advantageous. Third, neatly typed material, double-spaced is standard procedure. Who, what, where, when and how are the required lead elements of a satisfactory news story.

Columns: Billy Graham received 35,000 letters from persons every week. In response to that need, he initiated a daily advice column, "My Answer." It has gained a wide following for over a decade. The four to six inch, syndicated column gives Dr. Graham an enormous audience for regular evangelistic presentations.

Many small town weekly papers publish similar columns on their editorial pages by a local minister. Countless others would be open to such a consideration if they were approached on the matter. Such a writing ministry obviously gives any pastor a greatly multiplied audience over his own congregation. They also provided community awareness of the minister's concern.

Cartoons: The United Presbyterian Church's Presbytery has unveiled a new advertising campaign using "eye-catching cartoons." It intends to get more across to the reader than the place and time of Sunday services.

Jesus is portrayed through the cartoons in every situation. Charles Asay, a Presbyterian elder and artist draws the cartoons.

Rev. Raymond F. Kersting, chairman of the Denver Presbytery's advertising committee suggested in previous days they had used the paper for listing the United Presbyterian churches with the times of services. But they decided they must catch this type person's attention, and concluded that cartoons were the answer.

Kersting contended that the message is simple, but the "good News" character of the Gospel is communicated. He suggested that the message of Christ must be passed in every form, whether words, deeds or cartoons.

The cartoon feature entitled, "Insight"[1] appears every other week in the *Rocky Mountain News* religion section.

Books

Books are another force with the potential for evangelism and church growth. History abounds with people who were converted to Christ through reading matter. Augustine of Hippo was converted in the fifth century A.D. while reading the scriptures in his garden house. Dr. Carl Bates, past president of the Southern Baptist Convention was converted while reading a Gideon Bible in a hotel room.

Christian biographies, fiction, sermons and devotions have inspired the conversions of others. Books have been used in additional situations for a verbal Christian witness. Illustrations of this ministry are found in chapters four and six.

Christian Book Stores: Christian individuals and denominations are aware of the evangelistic and nurturing of books. The stated purpose of the Presbyterian Book Store at Omaha is to provide service for churches, pastors and individual Christians in their ministries.

A Christian shopping center developer planned a religious bookstore with an adjacent chapel in his complex. The chapel and bookstore were established with the intention of providing solace and hope to those in spiritual need.

Church Libraries: The Calvary Baptist Church of Garland, Texas, exhibited confidence in a book ministry in 1972. They dedicated a new resource center including a suite of rooms. This included a library of 4,000 volumes, an audio-visual library, a children's room, a reading corner and a work room.

No matter how outstanding church library selections may be — success depends on promotion. Southern Baptists have created The Associational Church Library Organization (TACLO) to assist churches in their task.

An attractive children's selection has potential for outreach. Children visiting the library may exert great influence over their loving parents to bring them again.

Religious selections may come from a variety of publishing companies. Significant sources for books include:

Abingdon Press, 201 Eighth Ave., S., Nashville, Tenn. 37202

Association Press 291 Broadway, New York, New York 10007

Baker Book House, 1019 Wealthy Street, S.E., Grand Rapids, Michigan 49506

Broadman Press, 127 Ninth Avenue, N., Nashville, Tenn. 37203

Convention Press, 127 Ninth Avenue, N., Nashville, Tenn. 37203

Harper and Row Publishers, 49 E. 33rd Street, New York, New York 10016

John Knox Press, Box 5, Downers Grove, Illinois 23209

Judson Press, Valley Forge, PA 19481

The MacMillan Co., 866 Third Avenue, New York, New York 10022

Fleming H. Revell Co., Old Tappan, New Jersey 07675

The Westminster Press, Witherspoon Building, Philadelphia, PA 19107

Zondervan Publishing House, 1415 Lake Drive, S.E., Grand Rapids, Michigan 49506

Bookmobiles: "People who have never heard of Southern Baptist are learning who we are and that we care,"[2] said Floyd Tidsworth, concerning church outreach through a bookmobile. In Wheeling, West Virginia, in the HIL DAR housing development there are 350 children and their parents. "Good books lent to them by people who care in the name of Christ are making a difference in the lives of these people who are hungry for someone to love them."[3]

The bookmobile ran Tuesday through Friday during afternoons and evenings. Several stations on the route were schools, grocery stores and community buildings. Church leadership met the people and developed friendships.

The "Good News Bookmobile" was a cooperative mission pilot project. The Home Mission Board purchased the vehicle and shelving.

The ministry was promoted with free TV, radio and newspaper announcements in the nine-county area. Leaflets were distributed in the beginning as to the schedule of the bookmobile.

This method can help enable the initiation of a mission in a community where no Baptists live.

Church Publications of Pastor's Messages: Ideally, a minister puts in over 20 hours a week in sermon preparation. The Westside Baptist Church of Omaha found a way to get maximum benefit from the pastor's studies.

The pastor, Rev. Calvin Miller made extensive studies of commentaries for a series of messages on the book of *Revelation*. His secretary typed a manuscript. Then a member in the congregation had the book, *The Omega Race,* printed. Copies were sold to members as well as friends of the Church. Young people responded to the book. It became a handy companion volume for the series on *Revelation*.

Magazines

In November, 1960, Billy Graham founded *Decision Magazine*. Exactly twelve years later the distribution became greater than *Life* Magazine, reaching 5.2 million persons per month. Graham said,

> I felt we needed a popular magazine that would go to the ordinary farm wife, to the worker, that would present clear Christian teaching, be thought-provoking, devotional and evangelistic with a breezy, easy-to-read style."[4]

The magazine's circulation grew from an initial 253,000 to over four million per month within nine years. It is now published in seven editions and five languages.

There are thirty-three Southern Baptist state papers which are of the nature of *Decision* magazine with sermons and news stories. Chief in circulation is the Texas *Baptist Standard* with over 375,000 subscribers.

Mail-Outs

Six days a week an employee of the U.S. Government visits every home in your city. He will deliver a message from your church to any home you desire for a small amount.

The administrative procedure for initiating a mail-out ministry includes: First, secure a third class mailing permit for $30 annually. Second, register as a non-profit organization (POD Form 3624, no fee) for a 50% discount on third class mailings. The rate in 1972 was one and a half cents per newsletter at this bulk rate. Third, pay postage by: (a) Meter stamps with proper license (POD Form 3601-A, no fee). (b) Pre-canceled stamps or pre-canceled envelopes (POD Form 3620, no fee). (c) Permit imprints (POD Form 3601, one time fee of $15).

Follow-Up On Telephone Survey: There are follow-up steps in the Home Mission Board *Urban Church Survey Manual* and the Sunday School Board's *People Search Guide*. The secret of the program's success is greatly dependent on an adequate follow-up. Mail-outs have a significant role in the procedure. There are mailings that come at specified intervals over a period of ten weeks. There letters cultivate a friendship and express personal concern.

Holiday Scripture Mailings: DeLane Ryals is a Church Extension consultant for the Metropolitan Baptist Association in New York City today. When he formerly served as a New Jersey Baptist pastor he sent each resident in his community a portion of the Scriptures with an announcement of special services at Christmas or Easter. The American Bible Society provided attractive publications of Scripture passages suitable for mailing at less than five cents each.

Letter to Prospects From Laity: The Exchange Baptist Church in Oklahoma City enlisted members to send special mailings to prospects. The names of prospects were distributed in Sunday School classes. The members received a pictoral folder, a letter to sign along with the prospects.

Names of new community prospects may be secured from the utility department, professional list, Welcome Wagon and criss-cross telephone directories.

Effective mailings include a clear explanation of the specified program. Clarity, friendliness and conciseness are essential. Also a method of response is vital. This may include a return card, or a name and telephone number to call.

The Public Relations Director of the Christian Life

Commission suggests the following guidelines for mail-outs:

Step One — Plan for each mailing at least one year in advance.

Step Two — Budget for all mailings; Learn to use postage permits.

Step Three — Use proved direct mail methods:

Know exactly what you want your mailing to do for you. It must have an objective.

Write your copy so the recipient will know what you will do for him.

Address correctly.

Make the layout and format tie in with the overall plan.

Make it easy to respond.

Tell your story over again and again.

Research the results.

Tracts

John B. McBride formerly of the Southern Baptist Convention Home Mission Board tells of the reaction of a youth at Ocean City, New Jersey, when he was handed a religious tract, "Is that all you have to give? If it is, I don't want it."[5]

McBride's conclusion was that distributing literature is second best to personal conversations. He also stressed that most tracts deal with salvation. Responsible tract distribution calls for offering a wide selection concerning all major issues and all of man's contemporary needs.

The diversity of tract subject matter enables a church to prepare the soil, plant the seed, cultivate the plant and harvest the crop.

Distribution centers should be set up wherever people go — hotel and motel lobbies, campground washrooms, hospital waiting rooms, newsstands, restaurants, laundromats and county fair booths.

The Delaware Valley Baptist Association rented a booth at the New Jersey State Fair. The Mississippi Baptist Convention did the same thing in its state. An Arkansas church distributes tracts at a mountaineer festival where it rents a booth.

The Lost and Found Coffeehouse in Worcester, New Hampshire, providesd tracts to attending young people.

The name and telephone number of the pastor or designated church leader should be stamped on the back for the sake of follow-up.

Among the key tract publishers, Mr. McBride lists the following:

Evangelistic Tracts
   Tract Editor, Sunday School Board, 127 Ninth Avenue, N., Nashville, Tenn. 37234
   Home Mission Board, 1350 Spring Street, Atlanta, Ga. 30309
   Peak Publications, Box 1210, Colorado Springs, Col. 80901

Education and Career
   Student Department, Sunday School Board, 127 Ninth Avenue, N., Nashville, Tenn. 37234
   Education Commission, SBC, 460 James Robertson Parkway, Nashville, Tenn. 37219.
   American Tract Society, Oradell, New Jersey 07649
   Inter-Varsity Fellowship, 1024 Warren, Downers Grove, Ill. 60515.

Ethics
   Christian Life Commission, 460 James Robertson Parkway, Nashville, Tenn. 37219

Scripture Portions
   American Bible Society, 1865 Broadway, New York, N.Y. 10023.

Correspondence Bible Courses

Several years ago Rev. James Wright, pastor of Highland Avenue Baptist Church in Queens, New York, wrote a letter to all the parents of children in his day care programs. He wrote, "I have been racking my brain to decide what to get you for Christmas." He offered the parents the free Home Mission Board correspondence Bible course. There were over one hundred responses from interested, unchurched parents.

The Evangelism department offers this Evangelistic course for the following purpose, "To proclaim Jesus the Lord and Saviour and urge people everywhere to experience a redeeming encounter with Him by faith and repentence."

The course is furnished to anyone who desires help in studying the Bible. It is primarily designed for people who have never had college or seminary Bible courses.

The study includes:

Ten lessons on the Gospels.

Ten lessons on Acts and NT Epistles.

Five lessons on the Pentateuch.

Five lessons on the historical books of the OT.

Eight lessons on the Poetical Books.

Six lessons on the Major Prophets.

Four lessons on the Minor Prophets.

HOW THE CHURCH GETS STARTED

The loftiest catalogue of ministries is worthless unless the church has a designated strategy for launching the efforts. Fortunately, Baptist churches have an abundance of organizations through which they may implement their diverse ministries.

The key layman in an organization may initiate an exciting ministry on his own volition. In other instances the pastor will meet with his Church Council to decide which organization is the most appropriate for beginning a needed ministry. This consultation between the pastor, Sunday School Director, Church Training Director, W.M.U. Director, Brotherhood Director, and Music Director should offer a harmonious solution to the best possible means of launching the ministry.

Perhaps, each organization will be deliberately searching for a ministry at different times. One group may be more ideally suited to employ the activities because of personnel, interests, or membership strength.

Consider five avenues a local church might pursue in order to initiate caring ministries to troubled and dejected persons:

Sunday School

Ministry should be as vital through the Sunday School as any other organization of the church. In the Sunday School there is an Outreach Director to coordinate visitation and ministries in the largest church organization. There is also an outreach specialist for every unit of people within the Sunday School, both departments and classes.

The Department Outreach Leader directs the overall

evangelistic efforts in his area, including the efforts of his Class Outreach Leaders. In every adult class there are Group Leaders. Each Group Leader serves as a minister to five to seven class members and unchurches prospects.

The Group Leader expresses concern when someone in his flock of members is absent or when he learns of his responsibility for cultivating an unchurched person. The Group Leader also has the opportunity to assist the members of his group in finding an outlet for their love through a tangible ministry. The Outreach Leader is able to correlate the endeavors with the Group Leaders.

Therefore, a Sunday School class of 25 adult women includes 25 potential layministers. This class would have four or five Group Leaders, as well as an Outreach Leader.

Ideally, the Outreach Leader will give an emphasis to the fact that God has given gifts for each person to use in ministry. Paul itemized the variety of gifts of the Spirit in Romans 12:6-8, 1 Corinthians 12:4-10, and Ephesians 4:11-12.

Each class member should be brought to the realization that he has such talents and abilities from God that should be utilized in ministry. Even vocational skills and hobby interests can enable individuals to share their faith in Christ to troubled community residents.

The Class Outreach Leader can meet with the Group Leaders to initiate a class strategy of suggesting potential ministries to the members. The ideal approach is to divide a blank sheet of typing paper into three vertical columns. In the center column the names of class members should be listed by the group of which they are a part. Besides the member's name, the leaders should itemize key gifts, talents, abilities or interests of the person.

In the left column the Outreach and Group Leaders should list unchurched persons on the class role whose problems or needs correspond to the gifts or abilities of members. Each prospect should be listed beside a bonafied class member. Even if the class member is not active, the concept of ministry might capture his imagination and awaken his participation. The prospect's need or interest should be written beside his name in the left margin.

The class leaders will suggest potential ministries in the right-hand margin beside the class member's names. One prospective ministry should be listed beside the name of each class member.

Members should be led to realize that Christian growth depends as much on sharing one's faith, as on prayer and Bible study. This type of class ministry provides members with such an opportunity to grow in Christlikeness.

CHURCH OUTREACH MINISTRY PLAN SHEET

NEEDS	MEMBER WITH ABILITY TO MEET THE NEED	SPECIFIC MINISTRY
(Specific Need of a person near the church building)	(Lay Minister with matching gift or ability)	(Class Member will begin this project)
Mrs. Arnold can't afford to clothe 6 kids.	Sara sews well. (Inactive).	Tue. afternoon sewing class for mothers.
Mrs. Smith needs to lose 48 pounds	Janie lost 45 pounds in Weight Watchers.	Mon. night Weight Watcher's class.
Mrs. Kendall has 3 preschool age children.	Ruth loves to work with kids (Inactive).	Wed. morn. child care service for children.
Llynn and Janet want to play golf.	Martha is a tournament golfer.	Mon p.m. golf class.
Mrs. Larson, Mrs. Cox can't live on income.	Loretta is a financial secretary.	Sat. p.m. Family Finance class on budget planning.

GROUP II MEMBERS

Mrs. Gibbs is bored and lonely all day.	Claudia makes ceramics (Inactive).	Fri. morn Ceramics class.
Mrs. Phillips and Mrs. Ryan work with Louise, don't attend church.	Louise is a secretary in an office building.	Monday lunch hour Bible Study Fellowship in office lunch room.
The Bolins, the Boyds, and the Morrises are new neighbors of Sandra.	Sandra's kids are in school, and she has time to help the church.	Friday morn tour of city and luncheon for newcomers to the city.
Mrs. Jennings can't read, but wants to.	Betty was English major and is taking Labach literacy course (Inactive).	Thurs. evening Literacy Class for adults who can't read.
Sally and Linda need help in grooming and selecting clothing.	Jenny is a beautician (Inactive)	Tues. p.m. Grooming Class for teen girls.

GROUP III MEMBERS

Bob, Sally, Cara, and Chris are kids with nothing to do after school.	Brenda loves children, and has big backyard (Inactive).	Fri. a.m. Backyard Bible Study with arts and crafts for kids.
Mrs. Adams is a lonely shut-in.	Barbara is a caring person with free time to help others.	Morning ministry to shut-ins with cassette tapes of sermons.
Bridges, Garza, and Green families are unchurched, and unknown.	Janet has done sales work over the telephone (Inactive).	Special Telephone Survey project.
Carol is lonely with her mother dead.	Peggy and her husband love children, and have none.	Big Sister program to help motherless girls.
Mrs. Lane is desperate with unfaithful husband.	Jennifer was a psychology major and is a good listener (Inactive).	Weekday morning Telephone Counseling Service for troubled people.

GROUP IV MEMBERS

The Martins need help in family planning.	Marie is a nurse who would like to help people with her medical insight (Inactive).	Tue. night Planned Parenthood meetings at church.
Mrs. Jones is an alcoholic wanting help.	Doris is a dry alcoholic who wants to help others.	Thurs. night Alcoholics Anonymous meetings.
Mrs. Dawson wants to start a garden.	Carla has a successful garden.	Sat. p.m. Gardening Club.
Mrs. Parks needs to get more exercise.	Lynn works at a health spa.	Tue. night ladies' exercise class.
Mrs. Higgins wants tips on beautifying her lawn.	Paula works for a landscaping company.	Wed. p.m. Landscaping Class (after church).

GROUP V MEMBERS

Mrs. Stephens is a widow who needs help with income tax report.	Linda works for the Internal Revenue Bureau.	Friday morn class on preparing income tax reports.
Mrs. Compton needs a lawyer, but can't afford one.	Susan is an attorney who is concerned for the poor.	Sunday p.m. legal aid service for needy.
Mrs. Glass is lonely and would like to knit.	Dorothy knits sweaters.	Mon. a.m. Knitting Class.
Mrs. Glover is lonely and likes chess.	Blanche is a chess and checker player.	Wed. a.m. Chess Club.
Janet is age 10, and is having trouble in school.	Peggy is a Math teacher.	Tutoring Class in Math on Tue. evenings.

Appealing To the Best In the Other Person

People are moved by a variety of motives — love, fear, guilt, hate. Sometimes believers have been guilty of appealing to a person to become a Christian through fear of hell. When this has happened, the church has tried to reach a man through his lower motives.

There is a better way! We can appeal to his highest motives! The call for help touches a person's sensitivity and compassion for others. Almost everyone responds to a cry for help. At least we comply if the request is made to us in a personal way, and if we recognize the need to be valid.

The Missions Committee

Many churches have discovered that the Missions Committee is an ideal vehicle through which to carry out ministries and programs that seem relevant to the community. The following six steps are recommended if the church operates their efforts through the Missions Committee:

A group of concerned individuals should be formulated to gather for planning mission strategy. Ideally, a church has a missions committee of six to eight people to assist the church in discovering and meeting local opportunities to minister. Even a church of less than a hundred members may involve the leaders of the missionary organizations and another person as chairman to form a Missions Committee. This committee also serves to correlate joint projects in which the Baptist men and women work together.

This mission strategy group discovers needs and determines approaches to meet the needs. The priority concern for the committee is a thorough analysis of community needs which might provide an opportunity for ministry.

In making a survey of community needs, the Missions

Committee can enlist additional help. The Associational Missions Committee may have significant resource information about the community. Municipal and county planning boards are helpful. Public welfare and employment agencies have pertinent data that will be useful to the committee. Counseling services at schools, hospitals, and social service agencies should provide additional data.

The worksheet opposite this page may be useful for the committee.

Every discovery of human need will suggest a potential ministry. Any evidence of blind, deaf or retarded persons in the community are opportunities for helping services by the congregation. The presence of alcoholics and drug addicts provide similar occasions for the church to give tangible expressions of love.

The Missions Committee may learn of others who are economically disadvantaged. A 1975 governmental survey indicated 20 percent of all American adults are unable to read or write. This suggests the enormous potential for such a local church ministry. Working mothers are ever-increasing and indicate a variety of prospective church programs. Both unwed mothers and couples on the brink of divorce are target groups for church labors.

After the human needs have been discovered, the Missions Committee devises and launches the ministry that is appropriate.

The Missions Committee may begin with this book to find suggestions for a caring response through ministry. The committee will want to initiate activities gradually in order to insure the success of each. However, a daring congregation will venture into as many avenues of service as possible.

The Church Council will seek to coordinate the Missions Committee plans with the total church program, and recommend them for congregational approval.

The Church Council may discern that the W.M.U. or

HUMAN NEED ON CHURCH FIELD

I. Human Problems	Illustrations of Problem	Needs Our Church Might Meet	Contact Person
1. Working Mothers			
2. People of another language or race			
3. Migrants			
4. Economically disadvantaged			
5. Illiterates			
6. Blind			
7. Deaf			
8. Crippled			
9. Retarded			
10. Alcoholics			
11. Drug addicts			
12. Ex-prisoners			
13. Children needing tutoring			
14. Juvenile delinquents			
15. Unwed mothers			
16. Sick			
17. Aging			
18. Problem families			

Brotherhood organizations can supply significant help in implementing the project. The Missions Committee might zero in on a ministry to the children in a high rise apartment complex. Individuals in the men and women's organizations are logical lay personnel to carry out the innovative plans.

But the Church Council may discern that the Sunday School, Church Training or Youth Choir would make the greatest contribution in other situations.

The congregation reviews the recommendations and adopts church goals and strategies to meet the goals. When the dream of the Missions Committee expands and becomes the official dream of the whole congregation, the broadened base of support strengthens the effort. The more persons who are involved in the planning and employment of a ministry increases the impact it will make.

The congregation's involvement in the early stages will insure total sympathy, if not increased participation in the endeavor.

The Missions Committee proceeds to administer and oversee the implementation of the ministry. If the Missions Committee is designated to enact the determined mission projects, it has a variety of responsibilities. The committee will need to secure leaders for the projects, find necessary materials, determine th time for the activity, and enlist participants who need the ministry.

The Missions Committee begins implementation of the actual ministries. The Missions Committee supervises the programs after all preliminary preparations have been completed. The committee is ever alert to support and encourage the designated leaders in carrying out their responsibilities. The Missions Committee is able to provide the constant reminder that the ultimate purpose of caring ministries is to bring men to God through Jesus Christ. Apart from this ever present reminder the ministries may tend to get out of focus and become ends in themselves.

The Women's Missionary Union

The Women's Missionary Union has two adult groups that major on mission action projects — Baptist Women and Baptist Young Women. Each organization has a Missions Action chairman who is the catalyst for sparking the participation of mission-minded ladies. She coordinates the Mission Action groups within the organization with the Mission Action Group Leaders. Through the Mission Action Groups the women are able to minister and witness to persons in difficult circumstances or with crucial needs.

Mission action projects begin in a variety of ways. There may be a spontaneous response by members to a need. Or the ministry might be a follow-through effort to a study or prayer experience of the group. Another way that ministries are launched are in response to crises which develop. The fourth approach is when Mission Action groups take an organized approach to determining community needs, and setting priorities to respond to those needs.

The Mission Action chairman leads in planning and conducting projects. The ministry may be conducted by the Mission Prayer Group or the Mission Study Group, as well as the Mission Action Group. The Mission Action Group Leaders lead in conducting those projects that they will employ.

Most coordination for the work of Baptist Women or Baptist Young Women is done by the officer's council. The Mission Action chairman offers her leadership through the council.

There are four basic steps in the planning and evaluating of Mission Action projects by Baptist Women: (1) A project is chosen after a purpose for the ministry is determined. (2) The actions are determined that are necessary to carry out the projects; (3) The project of ministry and witness is actually conducted; (4) The group evaluates the success of the project.

The Women's Missionary Union and the Brotherhood share

a series of Mission Action Group guides with purposeful projects in response to needs. There are guides for the following areas: Aging, Alcohol and Drug Abuses, Combating Moral Problems, Economically Disadvantaged, Headliners, Internationals, Juvenile Rehabilitation, Apartment Dwellers, Language Groups, Military, Negroes, Resort Areas, Non-Readers, Prisoners, The Sick, Projects Guide.

The Brotherhood

The Brotherhood organization is coordinated by a five man planning council. It is composed of a President, Vice-President and Secretary. These three may be combined in a small church. The other strategic officers are the Mission Study Leader and the Mission Activity Leader.

It is the Mission Activity Leader who assists in conducting a survey of mission action needs for the church. This leader provides mission action opportunities, as well as mission support groups for Baptist men. This Mission Activity Leader also coordinates the ongoing mission actions groups, as well as short-term projects.

The Mission Action Groups provide an opportunity for men to engage in mission service through small units. Generally, the men are enlisted for a project that corresponds to their talents or interests.

The Mission Action Groups utilize the same sixteen group guides that are listed above under the Women's Missionary Union.

Additional information concerning the duties of the Mission Activity Leader is included in *Baptist Men In Missions*, available from the Brotherhood Departments of the Baptist state conventions.

Church Training

The key person to spark ministry among individuals in the Church Training program is the Adult Training Group Application Leader. He has the task of helping members discover ways to apply to life the insights from the group studies. Following a study on the Good Samaritan, the Application Leader would assist the group in finding ways the members may express compassion to others. The Leader may select individual, as well as group projects.

The Application Leader will familiarize himself with other ministries and activities of the church through which group members may express their convictions in projects related to the mission of the church.

Suggested application activities for each unit are included in *Baptist Adult, Church Training* (first month of the quarter), *Young Adults In Training* and *Source*. The September, 1975, issue of *Church Training* deals with Job Training Guidelines for Church Training Leaders. Included in this issue is a section on Job Training Guidelines for the Adult Training Group Application Leader.

A helpful tool for the Application Leader would be to divide a blank sheet of paper into three vertical columns. The left hand margin should be for itemizing needs. Three sub-headings are listed beneath the main heading — church, community and family. The center column is for listing a description of an activity to meet the needs in the left margin. The right hand margin is for a list of resources that will be necessary to implement the ministry.

APPENDIX

(References whereby the reader may obtain additional information and resources for implementing the previously listed cultivative ministries.)

II. ONE-TO-ONE, PERSON-TO-PERSON
  Telephone
    Counseling
      Royal Service, February, 1971, p. 4.
      Church Administration, April 1971, p. 22.
      Marble Collegiate Church, New York, N.Y.
      FISH, Box 697, Hillsboro, Texas 76645
      Take It To the People, Howard E. Mumma (World Books), p. 110-111.
    Crises Center
      Rev. Robert Tremaine, First Baptist Church, Miami Beach, Florida.
    Follow-Up to Television
      North Phoenix Baptist Church, Phoenix, Arizona.
    Telephone Survey
    Urban Church Survey Manual, Home Mission Board, 1350 Spring St., Atlanta, Ga. 30309.
    Royal Service, July 1973, p. 25.
    People Search Guide, Kenneth Dean, (Convention), p. 24-30, 40-46.
    Prayer Service
    Recorded Devotionals
      Church Administration, February, 1973, p. 12-14.
      Church Administration, August, 1971, p. 16-18.
      Outreach For Children, Muriel Blackwell (Convention) Belmont Heights Baptist Church, Nashville, Tenn.
    Referrals
      FISH, Box 697, Hillsboro, Texas 76645

Personal Services
  Medical
    Well-Baby Clinics
      WMU Mission Action Group Guide: Economically Disadvantaged
      First Baptist Church, Mt. Pleasant, S.C.
      Rev. J.D. Holt, 1705, Corinth, Dallas, Texas 75215
    Medical Clinic
      Royal Service, December, 1970, p. 18-22.
      WMU Mission Action Group Guide: Economically Disadvantaged
      Church Administration, September, 1971, p. 17-19.
      Dr. Dale Cowling, Second Baptist Church, Little Rock, Arkansas 72202.
      Dr. Cecil Sherman, First Baptist Church, Asheville, N.C.
    Cooperation With Community Health Agencies
      Rev. J.M. Oswalt, First Baptist Church, Hammond, La.
      Rev. Dale Cross, 2619 Cass Ave., Detroit, Mich. 48201.
      How To Use Community Resources In Mission Action (WMU)
    Planned Parenthood Clinic
      Rev. John Hawk, 1016 Crinella, Petaluma, CA 94552.
  Food Distribution
    Royal Service, May 1973, p. 18-19, 27.
    First Baptist Church, 16th and O St., Washington, D.C.
    Wake Forest Baptist Church, Winston-Salem, N.C.
    Outreach: God's Miracle Business (Broadman Press), Elvis Marcum, p. 116.
  Housing
    Youth Facility

Rev. James Wright, 87-10 162nd St., Jamaica, N.Y., 11432.

Family Provisions
Rev. Kenneth Lyle, 236 W. 72 St., New York, N.Y. 10023.

Rev. Rodolph Morgan, 1245 Eastern Parkway, Brooklyn, N.Y. 11213.

Retirement Accomodations
Dr. Wayne Dehoney, 1101 S. Third, Louisville, Ky. 40203.

Legal
Rev. Edwin Armitage, 768 Smiley Avenue, Cincinnati, Ohio 45240.

Royal Service, February 1971, p. 9.

Rev. James Roamer, 636 Mangarita Ave., Coronado, CA 92118.

Educational
Tutoring
A Cup of Cold Water, Robert E. Bingham (Convention), p. 45.

Sounds of Christian Social Ministries (Broadman Recording)

Church Administration, June 1971, p. 23.

Royal Service, June 1971, p. 18019.

Summer Mission Action for Youth (SMAY) (Brotherhood), p. 34.

Outreach: God's Miracle Business (Broadman), Elvis Marcum, p. 79-85.

Literacy
Royal Service, September 1973, p. 16-17.

Accent, March 1971, p. 27-30.

Dr. Paul Adkins, Home Mission Board, 1350 Spring Street, Atlanta, Ga 30309.

Literacy Missions—A New Dimension (Broadman filmstrip).

Church Administration, November 1971, p. 28-30.
The New Streamlined English Series, Skill Books 1-5,
    Frank S. Laubach, Elizabeth Mooney Kirk, Robert S. Laubach (New Reader's Press), 1971.
Pattern Practices for the New Streamlined English Series, Teacher's Edition, Skill Boos 1, 2, 3.

Clothing
    WMU Mission Action Group Guide: Economically Disadvantaged
    Outreach: God's Miracle Business (Broadman Press), Elvis Marcum, p. 116.

Ministry to Newcomers
    Church Administration, March 1971, p. 29
    Outreach for Pre-Schoolers, Willa Ruth Garlow, p. 55.

Family Ministries
    Big Brothers—Big Sisters
    Outreach for Children, Muriel Blackwell, p. 11.
    Outreach for Pre-Schoolers, Willa Ruth Garlow, p. 17-18.
    Church Administration, April 1973, p. 31-34.

Vocational
    Church Administration, November 1971, p. 28.
    Rev. Elvis Marcum, 1734 Klerner Lane, New Albany, Indiana 47150.

III. SMALL GROUP APPROACHES
  Classes
    Household Hints
    Homemaking Demonstrations
      WMU Mission Action Guide: Economically Disadvantaged
      Miss Helen Neiger, Friendship House, Elysian Fields Ave., New Orleans, La.
    Nutrition

WMU Mission Action Guide: Economically Disadvantaged
Rev. Dale Cowling, Second Baptist Church, 222 E. 8th St., Little Rock, Arkansas 72202.
Rev. Don Weeks, 225 Cleveland St., Gary, Indiana 46404.
Cooking
WMU Mission Action Guide: Economically Disadvantaged.
Grooming
Royal Service, February 1971, p. 4.
Outreach: God's Miracle Business (Broadman), Elvis Marcum, p. 146.
Sewing
Royal Service, February 1971, p. 8.
The Touch of the Spirit, Ralph Neighbor, p. 85-86.
Wieuca Road Baptist Church, Atlanta, Georgia.
Health
Royal Service, May 1972, p. 1-2.
Exercise
  Nineteenth Ave. Baptist Church, San Francisco, CA.
Alcohol Treatment
    Alcoholics Anonymous
    Alcoholics Anonymous Organization
    WMU Mission Action Guide: Alcohol and Drug Abuse
    Bible Study
      Sagamore Hills Baptist Church, Ft. Worth, Texas.
Drug Treatment
    Gradual Withdrawal
    Home Missions, August 1970, p. 11-13.
    Dr. Ernest Gregory, Castle Hills Baptist Church, San Antonio, Texas.
    Immediate Withdrawal

Teen Challenge, New York City, New York
The Cross and the Switchblade, David Wilkerson.

Therapy Groups
Rev. Jim Redi, P.O. Box 932, Henderson, Nevada, 89015.
Yokefellows, Rev. Cecil Osborne, 209 Park Ave., Burlingame, Colorado.
Church Administration, October 1972, p. 10.
Church Administration, May 1972, p. 42.

Vocation
Church-Staffed and Sponsored Classes
Mechanics Class Rev. Elvis Marcum, Graceland Baptist Church, New Albany, Indiana.
Key-Punch Class
Rev. Larry Patterson, 914 N. Weatherly, Beverly Hills, CA.
Typing Class
Rev. Larry Patterson, 914 N. Weatherly, Beverly Hills, CA.
Church-Initiated Classes With Government Staffing
Rev. Ralph Longshore, 678 E. Shaw Ave., P.O. Box 5168, Fresno, CA 93755.
Church-Initiated Classes With Private Funding
Rev. Leon Sullivan, Zion Baptist Church, N. Broad Street, Philadelphia, PA.
Build, Brother, Build, Leon Sullivan.
Church Membership Classes
Encounter With Spurgeon, Helmut Thielecke, Fortress Press.
Church Administration, November 1972, p. 18.
Children's Education
Sesame Street Class, Children's Television Workshop, Public Television, New York, N.Y.
Miss Brenda Forlines, 1839 Finch Dr., Cornwell

Heights, Pennsylvania.
Head Start Classes
    Rev. Harold Parsley, Valley Baptist Church, San Francisco, CA.
    Department of Health, Education and Welfare, Washington, D.C.
Day Care Classes
    Church Administration, November 1971, p. 29.
    Church Administration, December 1972.
    Church Administration, March 1972, p. 37.
    First Baptist Church, Merchantville, New Jersey.
    Church Administration, June 1969, p. 14-20.
    Church Administration, November 1970, p. 26.
    Church Administration, June 1971, p. 20-23.
    Church Administration, March 19711, p. 34-35.
    Church Administration, January 1971, p. 39.
    Church Administration, February 1970, p. 30.
    Church Weekday Early Education (Teacher's Guide), Doris Haver Rouse, (Convention), 1972.
Drama
    Rev. Alvin Carmines, Judson Memorial Church, Greenwich, N.Y.
    Summer Mission Action for Youth (SMAY), *Brotherhood*, p. 61.
    Ideas for Youth Outreach, Billie Pate, p. 13.
    The Touch of the Spirit, Ralph Neighbor, p. 119-120.
Clubs
  Recreation
  Youth Lounge
    Rev. Richard Turner, St. Paul United Methodist Church, Omaha, Nebraska.
  Parents Without Partners

Church Administration, April 1973, p. 34-37.
A Cup of Cold Water, Robert E. Bingham, p. 42.
Hobby Classes
  Ceramics
    Rev. John Tanner, 854 Beach, S.E., Huron, S. Dakota 57350
  Chess
    Rev. Paul Baxter, Crittendon Baptist Church, Crittendon, N.Y.
  Quilting
    Calvary Baptist Church, Midland, Texas.
  Arts and Crafts
    Home Missions, June 1970, p. 37.
    Church Administration, July 1971, p. 37-40.
    Church Administration, June 1969, p. 12.
    Church Community Ministries (Broadman filmstrip)
  Photography
    Rev. Sam Satterfield, First Baptist Church, Corpus Christi, Texas.
  Dominoes
    Rev. Michael McDowell, 3000 W. Kellogg Dr., Wichita, Kansas.
  Skydiving
    Harrison Street Baptist Church, Omaha, Nebraska.
  Ham Radio
    Mr. Jerry Warfield, Bethel Baptist Church, Scottsbluff, Nebraska.
Athletics
  Weight Lifting
    Dr. John Hughston, 16 Beech St., Cambridge, Mass., 02140.
  Bowling
    Harrison Street Baptist Church, Omaha, Nebraska.
  Basketball

Chandler Acres Baptist Church, Omaha, Nebraska.
Rev. Harold Manahan, Hillcrest Baptist Church, Omaha, Nebraska.

IV. OTHER INNOVATIVE INDOOR MINISTRIES
Conversing
Bible Fellowship Study
Leading Coffee Dialogues (WMU)
Outreach for Children, Muriel Blackwell, (Convention), p. 32.
Night Club
Home Missions, February 1971, p. 3-6.
Rev. Jim Redi, P.O. Box 932, Henderson Nevada 89015.
Ranch Houses
Rev. Dewey Hickey, 110 E. 32nd St., South Sioux City, Nebraska 68776.
Business Building
Rev. Kenneth Lyle, 236 W. 72nd St., New York, N.Y. 10023.
Apartments
Apartment House Missionary (Broadman filmstrip)
Rev. Don Rhymes, Home Mission Board, 1350 Spring St., Atlanta, Ga. 30309.
City Homes
Extend Now: Organized Work (Broadman filmstrip)
Rev. F.J. Redford, Home Mission Board, 1350 Spring St., Atlanta, Ga. 30309.
Extend Now to All People (Broadman filmstrip)
Church Basement
Church Administration, January 1971, p. 36-37.
Rev. Larry Patterson, 914 N. Weatherly, Beverly Hills, CA.
Coffeehouses
Church Administration, June 1971, p. 12.

Home Missions, May 1971, p. 15-16.
Home Missions, October, 1970, p. 10-13.
The Coffee House Ministry, John Perry, John Knox Press.
Serendipity Books, Word
   Man Alive
   Acts Alive
   Celebration
Serendiptiy House, 1972
   Coffee House Itch
   Rap
   Breaking Free
   Beginnings
   Discovery
   Groups In Action
Church Administration, November 1971, p. 30-31.
   Beach House
      Church Administration, July 1972, p. 30.
      First Baptist Church, Lake Jackson, Texas.
   Village House
      Central Baptist Church, Lowesville, Virginia
   City House
      First Baptist Church, Bellevue, Nebraska 68005
   Storefront
      Rev. Duane McCormick, 5423 N. 61st Street, Omaha, Nebraska 61834.
   Church Basement
      Rev. Robert Tremaine, First Baptist Church, Miami Beach, Florida.
      Miss Brenda Forlines, 1839 Finch Drive, Cornwell Heights, PA 19020.
Studying
   Reading Room Concept
      Christian Science
   Library Ministry

Rev. Gordon Thomas, Box 733, Lewiston, Maine 04240

Rev. Floyd Tidsworth, 801 6th Ave., St. Abans, W.Va. 25177

Church Library Department, Sunday School Board, 127 Ninth Ave., North, Nashville, Tenn.

Book Store Ministry

Rev. Harry Bristow, Christian Cinema, Jenkintown, PA 19946

Book Review

Park Cities Baptist Church, Dallas, Texas

Outreach

Sunday School

Outreach Evangelism Through the Sunday School, Othal Feather

Outreach for Unenrolled Church Members (Broadman filmstrip)

A Sunday School Visitation Program (Broadman filmstrip)

Principles of Visitation (Broadman filmstrip)

Outreach Visitation (Broadman filmstrip)

Visiting the Unsaved (Broadman filmstrip)

Enlarging a Sunday School (Broadman filmstrip)

Vacation Bible School

Ideas For Adult Outreach, (Convention Press), p. 17-22.

The Challenge of Vacation Bible School (Broadman filmstrip)

Local Church Building

Administering a Vacation Bible School, A.V. Washburn, (Convention)

Ideas for Vacation Bible School Promotion, William R. Cox

The Challenge of Vacation Bible School (Broadman filmstrip)

Counseling
- Shopping Centers
    Rev. George Colgin, Assistant Clinical Director, Training Center State Hospital, Milledgeville, Ga. 31061.
- Race Track
    Mr. Mike Eyer, Southern Baptist Theological Seminary, 2825 Lexington Road, Louisville, Ky. 40206
    Home Missions, July 1970, p. 18-21.
- Apartment House
    Royal Service, March 1971, p. 27.
    Apartment House Missionary (Broadman filmstrip)
    Rev. Don Rhymes, Home Mission Board, 1350 Spring St., Atlanta, Ga. 30309
- Jails
    Royal Service, February 1971, p. 9-12.
    WMU Mission Action Guide: Prisoner Rehabilitation
    Chandler Acres Baptist Church, Omaha, Nebraska.
- Y.M.C.A.
    Rev. Robert Bell, P.O. Box 9886, Philadelphia, PA 19140
- Night Club
    Rev. Jim Reid, P.O. Box 932, Henderson, Nevada 89015
- Hotel
    Rev. John Hughston, 16 Beech St., Cambridge, Mass. 02140

Feeding
Royal Service, May 1973, p. 18-19, 27
WMU Mission Action Guide: Economically Disadvantaged

Performing
- Church Building
    - Style Show

Rev. Peter Lord, Park Avenue Baptist Church, Titusville, Florida 32780

Lounge
- Musical Presentation

  Rev. Frank Scott, P.O. Box 1762, Pittsburgh, PA 15230

  Summer Mission Action for Youth (SMAY), Brotherhood, p. 48-49.

Night Club

Mr. Pat Boone, Hollywood, CA. Rev. Bob Harrington, Box 2408, New Orleans, La. 70116

Playing

Shopping Center

Rev. Kenneth Lyle, 236 W. 72nd Street, New York, N.Y. 10023

Dr. Paul Adkins, Home Mission Board, 1350 Spring St., Atlanta, Ga. 30309

Rev. Dan Grubb, 4004 Woodworth Rd., Brookhaven, Pa. 19015.

Church Property

Miss Brenda Forlines, 1839 Finch Dr., Cornwell Heights, Pa. 19020.

Center

Royal Service, February 1971.

Rev. Duane McCormick, 5423 N. 61st St., Omaha, Nebraska.

Dr. Paul Adkins, Home Mission Board, 1350 Spring St., Atlanta, Ga. 30309

Worshipping

Motion Picture Theaters

Sermons Preached at the Palace, W.A. Criswell

Dr. W.A. Criswell, First Baptist Church, Dallas, Texas

Night Clubs

Rev. Bob Harrington, Box 2408, New Orleans, La. 70116

Shopping Centers
: Rev. Gordon Thomas, Box 733, Lewiston, Maine 04240

Race Track
: Horse Race
  : *Home Missions*, July 1970
: Race Cars
  : Rev. Bill Frazier, Darlington, S.C.

School Auditoriums
: High School
  : Rev. John Bisagno, First Baptist Church, 1020 Lamar St., Houston, Texas 77002
: College
  : Ashbury College, Wilmore, Kentucky.

V. CREATIVE OUTDOOR MINISTRIES

Recreation
: Neighborhood Recreation Program
  : *Outreach*, June 1970
  : *Mission Vacation Bible School Filmstrip*
  : *Mission Vacation Bible School Advance Planning Kit* (Convention)
  : *Backyard Bible Club — Ages 6-11* (Broadman)
  : *Backyard Bible Club* (Teacher's Book)
  : *Extend Now: Community Events* (Broadman filmstrip)
: Bible School at Catholic Site
  : *Home Missions* January 1973, p. 16-18
  : Rev. Ken Prickett, 2915 Bob Drive, St. Charles, Mo. 63301
: Ongoing Park Program
  : *Outreach for Children*, Muriel Blackwell, p. 38.
: Athletic Clinics
  : *Home Missions*, November 1970, p. 22-23.
: Race Track
  : *Home Missions*, July 1970

Camp Grounds
    Rev. Joel Land, Home Mission Board, 1350 Spring St., Atlanta, Ga. 30309
    Campfire Sing-a-Long
        Home Missions, July 1970
        Family Camping, Lloyd D. Mattson
    Motion Pictures
Beach Sharing
    Rapping Session Rev. Joel Land, Home Mission Board, 1350 Spring St., Atlanta, Ga. 30309
Day Camp
    First Baptist Church, Brunswick, Ga.
    Day Camp Director's Package (Indian) (Frontier)
    Units 1, 11 Leader's Package for Day Camping (Indian) (Frontier)
    Units 1, 11 Package for Day Camping (Frontier)
Youth Happening
    Piano Drop
        Rev. Bill Lewis, Dimension, Philadelphia, Pa.
    Ecology Rock Festival
        Rev. Jerry Edwards, 16 Beech St., Cambridge, Mass. 02140.
    Skating Party
        Rev. John Nichol, 1743 Ridgecrest Ct., N.E., Atlanta, Ga. 30307
    State Fair Performances
        Royal Service September 1969, p. 10-11
        Set the Church Afire, Wayne Dehoney
        Rev. G.W. Bullard, 900 S. Arlington Ave., Harrisburg, Pa. 17109
        Take It To the People, Howard E. Mumma, p. 65-68
Diverse Worship Approaches
    Beach
        Home Missions October 1970, p. 10-25
    Race Track

Home Missions July 1970, p. 18
Parking Lot
   Rev. Charles Hawley, First Baptist Church, Bellevue, Nebraska
   Rev. Robert Tremaine, First Baptist Church, Miami Beach, Florida
Encounter With Spurgeon, Helmut Thielecke (Fortress), p. 162-176
Golf Course
   Rev. Donald Davis, Sunrise Presbyterian Church, Miami, Florida
   LaHaina Baptist Mission, Maui, Hawaii
Marketplace
   Olivet Baptist Church, Waikiki, Hawaii
Shopping Center
   Trinity Baptist Church, Lexington, Kentucky
   Walnut Street Baptist Church, Louisville, Kentucky
Set the Church Afire, Wayne Dehoney
   Beverly Hills Baptist Church, Asheville, North Carolina
Home Missions, September 1970, p. 37
City Park
   Rev. Jack Smith, 424 Woodmont Rd., Johnstown, Pa. 15905
Take It To the People, Howard E. Mumma (World Books), p. 59
Drive-In Church
   Rev. Robert Schuller, Garden Grove Community Church, Garden Grove, California
   Pasadena Community Church, St. Petersburg, Florida
Drive-In Theater
   Rev. Robert Schuller, Garden Grove Community Church, Garden Grove, California
Take It To the People, Howard E. Mumma (World Books), p. 54

VI. MOBILE MINISTRIES
  Mobile "Transporting" Ministries
    Transportation to Church Services
      Rev. D. Lewis White, Sunday School Board, 127 Ninth Ave., N., Nashville, Tennessee
      Outreach, March 1971, p. 24-28
      Outreach, May 1973, p. 38-39
      Church Administration, February 1971, p. 30
      Church Administration, August 1971, p. 26-28
      Church Administration, June 1971, p. 42
      Church Bus Evangelism, Bill Powell, Church Growth Publications
      Bus Outreach Starter Kit (Broadman)
      Outreach With Church Buses (Convention)
      How To Build a Bus Ministry, James Coggin, B.M. Spooner
      Busing Ministry (Broadman cassette)
      Outreach Through Bus Ministry (Broadman filmstrip)
    Transportation "Taxi" Ministry
      Home Missions, October 1971, p. 28-31
    Transportation on City Tours
      First Baptist Church, 48 Meeting St., Charleston, South Carolina 29401
      Church Administration, July 1970, p. 27-29
    Transporting Parade Float Ministry
      Set the Church Afire, Wayne Dehoney
  Mobile "Performing" Ministries
    Puppet Shows
      Rev. Bob Kleinschmidt, First Baptist Church, Box 236, Lemon Grove, California 92045
    Ventriloquism and Movies
      Rev. Meredith Wyatt, 6201 Wible Rd., Bakersfield, California 93307
      Dimension, August 1973
    Gingerbread House

Child Evangelism Fellowship, Richmond, California
Mobile "Delivering" Ministries
  Books
    Rev. Floyd Tidsworth, 801 6th Ave., St. Abans, West Va. 25177
    James Rose, Sunday School Board, 127 Ninth Ave., N., Nashville, Tennessee
  Recreational
    Rev. Elvis Marcum, 1734 Klerner Lane, New Albany, Indiana 47150
Mobile Facility As a Meeting Place
  Branch Sunday School
    Rev. Elvis Marcum, 1734 Klerner Lane, New Albany, Indiana 47150
  Youth Bible Fellowship Study
    Woodlawn Baptist Church, Decatur, Georgia
  Trailer Park Activities
    Walnut Street Baptist Church, Louisville, Kentucky
    Set the Church Afire, Wayne Dehoney (Broadman Press)
  Worship Facility
    Rev. James Keyes, Highway Evangelist, Waterdown, Ontario
  Counseling Service
    Rev. Gordon Thomas, Box 733, Lewiston, Maine 04240

VII. NON-PERSONAL CONFRONTATIONS THROUGH ELECTRONICS

  Electronics
    Radio
      Outreach, April 1973, p. 21-23
      Church Administration, February 1973, p. 42-43
      Radio and Television Commission, 6350 West Freeway, Ft. Worth, Texas 76116
      Religious News

  Church Administration, October 1972, p. 43
  Church Administration, May 1970, p. 36-38
Devotionals
  Church Administration, August 1971, p. 12
Worship
Spot Announcements
  Royal Service, November 1972, p. 13
  Church Administration, August 1969, p. 26
  Royal Service, July 1971, p. 4-5
Panel Discussion
  Radio and Television Commission, 6350 W. Freeway, Ft. Worth, Texas
Music Presentations
Interviews
Television
  Radio and Television Commission, 6350 W. Freeway, Ft. Worth, Texas
    Home Missions Variety Programs, April 1973, p. 22-23; June 1973, p. 8-9
    Evangelism Department, Home Mission Board, 1350 Spring St., Atlanta, Georgia 30309
  Spot Announcements
    Church Administration, June 1972, p. 44
    Church Administration, May 1972, p. 32
  Dramatic Presentations
    Rev. Harry Bristow, Christian Cinema, Jenkintown, Pa. 19046
    Radio and TV Commission, 6350 W. Freeway, Ft. Worth, Texas
  Cartoons
    Radio and TV Commission, 6350 W. Freeway, Ft. Worth, Texas
    Outreach, April 1973, p. 22
  One Minute Sermon
    Rev. James Pletiz, 500 N. Palafox St., Pensacola, Fla. 32501

Worship Services
- *Church Administration*, October 1969, p. 18-19
- *Church Administration*, April 1973, p. 41-43
- *Church Administration*, November 1971, p. 23-25
- *Church Administration*, July 1973, p. 20-27

Secular Talk Shows
- Mike Douglas Shows, KYW, Walnut St., Philadelphia, Pa.

Motion Pictures
- Films for Occasional Church Showings
    - Broadman Films, Baptist Book Stores, Customer Accounts Center, 127 Ninth Ave., N., Nashville, Tennessee 37234
    - Billy Graham Evangelistic Assoc., Minneapolis, Minnestoa
- Film Revivals
    - Billy Graham Evangelistic Assoc., Minneapolis, Minnesota
- Films at Fair Pavillions
    - *Royal Service*, September 1969, p. 10-11
    - *Set the Church Afire*, Wayne Dehoney (Broadman)
- Films in Theaters and Auditoriums
    - Billy Graham Evangelistic Association
    - Gateway Films, American Baptist Convention, Valley Forge, Pa.
- Christian Films in Christian-Owned Theaters
    - Harry Bristow, Christian Cinema, Jenkintown, Pa. 19046
- Secular Films In Theaters
    - *Marque Ministries, The Movie Theater As Church and Community Forum*, Robert Konzelman

Computers
- *Church Administration*, January 1969, p. 32
- *Church Administration*, May 1969, p. 23

Church Administration, September 1969, p. 8
Church Administration, October 1969, p. 32
 Geographical Matching for Visitation
  Church Administration, November 1971, p. 40-41
  Church Administration, May 1971, p. 36
  Membership Services, Inc., Box 1207, Irving, Texas 75060
 Interest Matching for Visitation
  James W. Bryant, First Baptist Church, Dallas, Texas
  Royal Service, November 1971, p. 1-3
  Royal Service, November 1972, p. 8-10
 Cassette Tape Recordings
  Home Missions, November 1970, p. 13-18
  Church Administration, October 1970, p. 39-40
  Church Administration, June 1970, p. 38-39
Cassette Tape Recordings
 Home Missions, November 1970, p. 13-18
 Church Administration, October 1970, p. 39-40
 Church Administration, June 1970, p. 38-39
Inter-Communications System
 Selma Baptist Church, Johnston Association, North Carolina

VIII. NON-PERSONAL CONFRONTATIONS THROUGH LITERATURE

Literature
Newspapers
 Advertisements
  Christian Communicators Handbook, Floyd C. Craig (Broadman)
 News Stories
  Church Administration, October 1972, p. 43
  Church Administration, October 1970, p. 40-42
  Outreach, April 1973, p. 21

Church Administration, January 1969, p. 24
Church Administration, June 1972, p. 47-48
Columns
Church Administration, February 1969, p. 39
Royal Service, November 1972, p. 11-13
Cartoons
Religion in American Life (RIAL), New York, N.Y.
Books
Home Missions, June 1970, p. 30
Church Administration, July 1970, p. 36-37
Christian Book Store
Rev. Harry Bristow, Christian Cinema, Jenkintown, Pa. 19046
Church Libraries
Rev. Gordon Thomas, Box 733, Lewiston, Maine 04240
Church Administration, October 1972, p. 37
Church Administration, May 1971, p. 26
Bookmobiles
Rev. Floyd Tidsworth, 801 6th Ave., St. Abans, West Va., 25177
Church Publications of Pastor's Messages
Rev. Calvin Miller, 11929 Woolworth, Omaha, Nebraska 68144
Magazines
Decision Magazine, Minneapolis, Minnesota
Baptist Press, 460 James Robertson Parkway, Nashville, Tennessee 37219
Mailouts
Follow-up on Telephone Survey
Urban Church Survey Manual, Home Mission Board, 1350 Spring St., Atlanta, Ga. 30309
A Cup of Cold Water, Robert E. Bingham (Convention Press), 1971, p. 42

   Holiday Scripture Mailings
    Church Administration, February 1971, p. 22
   Letter to Prospects from Laity
    Church Administration, May 1972, p. 22
    Church Administration, June 1971, p. 34-36
  Tracts
    Church Administration, February 1971, p. 13-16
  Correspondence Bible Course
   Home Mission Board, 1350 Spring St., Atlanta, Ga. 30309

IX. HOW A CHURCH GETS STARTED

Associational Missions Committee (Broadman filmstrip)

Extend Now to All People (Broadman filmstrip)

Rev. F.J. Redford, Home Mission Board, 1350 Spring St., Atlanta, Ga. 30309

Extend Now: Organized Work (Broadman filmstrip)

Women's Missionary Union, 600 N. 20th St., Birmingham, Alabama 35203

Brotherhood, 1548 Poplar Avenue, Memphis, Tennessee 38104

FOOTNOTES

Chapter I

1 Graham, Billy, Southern Baptist Convention Address, June 7, 1972.
2 Ibid, Graham.
3 Metz, Graham, *New Congregations,* 1967, Westminster Press, Philadelphia, Pa.
4 *Home Missions Magazine*, July 1970, p. 8.
5 *Home Missions Magazine*, March, 1968, p. 7, 11.
6 Barclay, William, *Turning To God* (Philadelphia; The Westminster Press, 1964), p. 103.
7 Fanning, Buckner, Southern Baptist Convention Pastor's Conference, 1967.

Chapter II

1 W. Malcolm Fuller, *Church Administration*, May, 1967, p. 40-41.
2 Robert J. Norman, *Church Administration*, 1971, p. 17.
3 Howell, Robert, *Fish For My People*, (New York: Moorehouse Barlow Co., 1971), p. 33.
4 Ibid, Howell, p. 33.
5 *Home Missions Magazine*, January, 1971, p. 51.
6 *Royal Service*, Jan., 1968, p. 4.
7 *Home Missions Magazine*, August, 1967, p. 13.
8 Ibid, p. 14.
9 Dwayne Zimmer, *Church Administration*, February, 1968, p. 38.
10 *Royal Service*, February, 1971, p. 9.
11 *Home Missions Magazine*, January 1971, p. 20.
12 *Home Missions Magazine*, January, 1971, p. 20.
13 *Church Administration*, January 1972, p. 34.
14 Green, Bryan, *The Practice of Evangelism*, (Charles Scribner's Sons, 1951).

Chapter III

1 *Church Administration*, June, 1971, p. 24.
2 *Church Administration*, December, 1966, p. 34.
3 *Home Missions Magazine*, May, 1971, p. 30-31.
4 Wilkerson, David, *The Cross and the Switchblade*, p. 149, Old Tappan, N.J.: Fleming H. Revell Company, 1970.
5 Ibid, Wilkerson, p. 154.
6 Ibid, Wilkerson, p. 154.
7 Contempo, August, 1972, p. 47.
8 *Times-Picayune*, January 14, 1973.
9 Sullivan, Leon, *Build, Brother, Build,* p. 89, Philadelphia: Macrae Smith Company, 1969.
10 Ibid, Sullivan, p. 167.
11 Ibid, p. 171.
12 Thielicke, Helmut, *Encounter With Spurgeon*, p. 60, Philadelphia: Fortress Press, 1963.
13 *Newsweek*, April 7, 1969.

Chapter IV

1 *Royal Service*.
2 *The Light and Life*.
3 Barnett, J.N., *The Pull of the People*, (Nashville: Sunday School Board, 1959), p. 47.
4 Adcock, Joe. *Philadelphia Bulletin*.
5 *Home Missions Magazine*, May 1972, p. 48.
6 *Baptist Messenger*, July 27, 1972, p. 3.
7 *Home Missions Magazine*, June-July, 1971, p. 36

Chapter V

1 Knight, Walker, *Home Missions Magazine*, August, 1972, p. 24.
2 *Decision*, March, 1971, p. 14.

Chapter VI

1 Knight, Walker, *Home Missions Magazine*, August, 1972, p. 24.

Chapter VII

[1] Duncan, Clarence, *Church Administration*, May, 1972, p. 33.
[2] Duncan, Clarence, *Church Administration*, May, 1970, p. 37.
[3] Ibid, Duncan.
[4] Pollock, John, *Crusade* (Minneapolis: World Wide Publishers, 1969), p. 170.
[5] Ibid, Pollock, John, p. 241.
[6] Ibid.
[7] Ibid.
[8] *Church Administration*, February, 1968, p. 32.
[9] Ibid.
[10] Ibid.
[11] *Church Administration*, September 1970, p. 16.
[12] Ibid.
[13] Ibid.
[14] *Biblical Recorder*, July 29, 1972, p. 7.
[15] *Outreach*, October, 1972, p. 40.

Chapter VIII

[1] Henry, Carl, *Successful Church Publicity*, (Grand Rapids, Michigan, Zondervan, 1943).
[2] *Rocky Mountain News*, November 4, 1972, p. 126.
[3] Media Magazine, October-December, 1972 (Nashville: Sunday School Board), p. 8.
[4] Pollock, John, *Crusade* (Minneapolis: World Wide Publishers, 1969), p. 170.
[5] McBridge, Johnny, *Church Administration*, February, 1971, p. 13.

DATE DUE

FEB 25 '80	DE 06 '99
NOV 3 0 '80	
NOV 2 5 '80	
MAY 1 2 '81	
MAY 27 '81	
DEC 1 4 '81	
JAN 2 5 '83	
DEC 2 3 '83	
DEC 2 3 '83	
MAR 26 '86	
FEB 16 '87	
AUG 3 '87	
JA 09 '90	
DE 10 '90	
MR 11 '92	
NO 30 '96	

DEMCO 38-297

BV
3790
P656

Potter, C   Burtt.
    The church reaching out / Burtt Potter ; foreword by Owen Cooper. — Durham, N.C. : Moore Pub. Co., c1976.
    164 p. ; 24 cm.
    Includes bibliographical references.
    ISBN 0-87716-062-7 : $5.00

14744

HIEBERT LIBRARY
Pacific College - M. B. Seminary
Fresno, Calif. 93702

1. Evangelistic work.   I. Title.

BV3790.P656   269'.2   76-12219
                                                                                                          MARC

Library of Congress   76